THE MIGRANTS CAREER GUIDE

PROVEN STEPS TO RELAUNCH YOUR CAREER IN A NEW COUNTRY

BANJI ALO

CONTENTS

PREFACE

The Migrants Career Guide was written based on my experience and interaction with fellow migrants.

To Timi and Toba

INTRODUCTION

Thank you for picking up a copy of my book. I am guessing you are either a new or prospective migrant or have some interest in migration. If you are, then you are at the right place.

Seven years ago, when I moved from Nigeria to Australia, I did not imagine that I would have written to find a career guidance book for migrants. But here we are today; I have just done that for you.

WHY THIS BOOK?

I have shared this guide to assist you in navigating through the complex challenges migrants face when establishing themselves in a new country.

Indeed, moving from a country where you grew up with all your family, friends, and neighbours to a new country where you barely know anyone is a big change. Not only should you adjust to the unfamiliar weather, culture, food, travel, language, and everything else you find in the destination country, but you must also develop your career. That is why I have written this book.

I have firsthand experience of how the careers of migrants are shaped and how they struggle when they relocate from their home country to a foreign land with the aim of establishing a better life or enhancing their family's living conditions. If you are one such professional, then you have made the right decision to buy a copy of this book. This book will be worth every penny!

This guide will help you overcome the early career challenges and relaunch your career in your destination country.

I have organised this guide into various sections that are

linked to one another. The information in each part flows into the next part. I recommend you not to skip any part but read the entire book to understand what you, being a migrant, need to succeed in your career.

What you will learn

The first part presents an introduction to setting things up in your new destination country before you arrive or as you arrive. You may already know some things in this regard, but it is always a good idea to review them so you do not miss any important elements. The actual preparations required for moving to a new country may also vary depending on your destination country, but the approach is similar irrespective of which country you have chosen to migrate to and relaunch your career.

In the second part, we discuss the survival path. As a migrant, I have seen and experienced firsthand how migrants fulfil their career goals while navigating the early challenges of survival. Migrants often take up casual jobs during the early stages of their migration for survival. These jobs can provide both advantages and disadvantages in terms of long-term career goals. This part explains how casual jobs can be turned into a stepping stone towards a career of choice.

In the third part of this book, we discuss the option of returning to school for a new migrant. Sometimes, this option becomes visible if you need local education to add to your portfolio or quickly gain knowledge in a specific field of interest. I will discuss what benefits returning to school offers, whether it is the right move for you, and what other alternatives exist to enrolling in an expensive and time-consuming degree.

In the fourth part of this book, we discuss the steps you need to follow to continue working in your original profession. Yes, it is possible to land a role in your destination country in the same field you had worked where you originally lived. Here, we go over what information you must know, how to navigate the early challenges you might face when applying to a job, and the best approach to landing any role you want.

In part five, we discuss how you can become your own boss by using the skills you already have and offering services to your community and the world. Maybe you do not need a job at all. You never know. Perhaps you can be your own boss, solve problems in your community, and enjoy the satisfaction, freedom, and creativity of an entrepreneur.

We wrap up the book with the sixth and final part that offers tips to help you stay motivated. It highlights the uniqueness of each migrant's path. It touches upon the importance of finding a mentor and seeking help when needed. Lastly, it emphasises that you must do your own research to understand the job market and the trends in your field to build a successful career.

Remember to stick around to the end to learn how you can claim your free gift.

Who the book is for?

This book is for prospective or current migrants, especially those from low- and middle-income countries who are moving to a more advanced country.

Some of the concepts will also be helpful to migrants moving between two Western societies.

This book will also assist individuals who are already established in a new land. The content will help them achieve their career goals as well as provide quality career advice to fellow migrants who may approach them for guidance.

PART I

WELCOME HOME!

A friend of mine popularly used the term "home" when chatting. In the initial stages, I became confused as I could not understand whether he meant his country of birth or the new country he lived in. As it happens, he refers to his new country as "home".

So, welcome home!

If you are new to your destination country, I welcome you! This is a big change that I know you have worked hard to achieve. You probably resigned from your job back home and disposed of your belongings to move to your new country.

You have arrived full of expectations of a better life and want to hit the ground running as soon as possible. Your plans and vision are valid. We all deserve a better life.

So, while you are busy unpacking your suitcases, waiting to launch into the world and make a mark in your career, it is important to get the basic things done. This is nothing but getting access to essential services that you need to relaunch your career.

At this stage, I assume that you have obtained a local

mobile number. If you haven't done so, you want to do that as soon as possible because you will need to provide your mobile number when you register for local services.

I also assume that you have found an accommodation. This is crucial. Because you need an address to be able to receive important notices and letters. Perhaps you did not have a local postal service in your country. Things are about to change now. You will receive many paper notices, so finding accommodation as soon as possible is a top priority.

Managing your money

Now that you have a working local phone number and a roof over your head, your next step is to complete the work related to your bank accounts and tax registrations. If you have migrated from a country without a strict tax law, prepare for change.

Most advanced countries, including the one you are currently in, have strict tax laws. And one thing you must avoid is facing issues with government officials due to financial matters.

So, head to the government taxation office website and complete the necessary form to obtain your personal tax identification number. The name of this number will vary depending on the country you are in. For example, in Australia, it is called Tax File Number (TFN).

You will be required to provide this information during recruitment. If you are an employee, your taxes will be deducted automatically from your wages, and your company will pay this tax to the government. If you intend to run your own business, you need to register your business/company first.

Of course, to receive payments, you need to open a local bank account as soon as possible. If you are unsure which bank would best suit you, you can ask local friends or new connections to recommend. You can then choose a bank based on its services and features.

Accessing local resources

You will likely find and join local community groups as well. This may be a denomination of a religious body you belonged to back home or a community of people with the same background and culture. Having such a support network will help migrants feel less isolated, especially in the initial days. By interacting with those with a common language or shared interests and values in a foreign land and learning their experiences, you will be able to adapt more easily to the new environment.

While it is easy to ask people around you for information, doing your research first may help you find information that may be readily available online. If you do your research and put in some effort to source information, it would be easier for someone to answer a question or two from you rather than spending 2 to 3 hours explaining the entire process to you.

Generally, countries that take migrants make basic information resources available to them for free. This information can easily be accessed online. Check out the official websites of government agencies. These official websites are the most authentic places where migrants can find helpful and useful information.

Once you have done all this, you can learn about the local job websites related to your industry, especially if you are seeking a job. Visit websites of companies that are well-known and have a good reputation to view job openings. Familiarise yourself with the local job market. Most countries have popular job boards. I highly recommend that you register on these websites and install the mobile app version of these job boards on your mobile phone. You can conduct job searches, save your preferences for your preferred job roles, and create email alerts. That way, you do not have to check these sites for new job postings continuously.

You may already know most of these facts, but I have covered them as these are the essential first steps in job hunting. We will discuss resume writing and other steps at length in later chapters.

Actions:

- Familiarise yourself with local job boards.
- Create an account on these websites and add your data.
- Install mobile app versions of these job websites, if available.
- Create alerts for your preferred job roles.

START WITH WHY

This is a subject that I include in almost all my books.

Why?

You will need to revisit your *why* at every point while navigating your career. Reestablishing your *why* is important for you to understand why you are here and to help you keep focussed on that reason.

You probably defined your goals before you moved to your new country, but now is the time to do so again to refine them.

Neglecting your *why* at any point can lead to failure. You must hold strongly to your *why* so as not to forget why you made the big move.

Understanding your why will help you navigate the challenges in your new country. It will help you to stay on track and ensure you keep pursuing your goals, desires, aspirations and dreams.

Your *why* will help you stay motivated, so you are not discouraged when things do not work your way, especially in the early days. Knowing why you are here will keep you going and help you bounce back after facing disappointments.

Yes, you will likely encounter some bottlenecks along the

way. I faced these challenges and have seen many other migrants like you experience challenges when settling in a new country.

These challenges are expected, and almost everyone has experienced them. So, do not feel like there's something wrong with you and your decision to migrate to a new land. Moreover, you probably experienced failures and rejections in your home country. Instead of seeing these as setbacks, see them as opportunities to learn from mistakes and fine-tune your strategy.

You will need your *why* when you are about to give up on your dreams. This will remind you to keep pushing amidst hardship.

You will need your *why* when you are low on energy and require your inner strength to give you another push. Your *why* will be there to lift you and provide you with the energy you need to move ahead.

You would need your why to persist in your life's journey. Life is not a race; it is a journey. And yours is unique to you. Your job is to ensure that you are better than where you used to be and that you remain focused on achieving your goals.

Your why will help you focus on your career goals by helping you make the best use of your limited resources, especially in the early days. Yes, your money and time are particularly limited, so you want to ensure you are spending these resources towards actions or activities that lead to your goals.

Life is not about comparison; do not compare your career to that of other migrants. Focus on your *why* and your career goals and work towards them.

You will need your *why* when it seems all hope is lost and there is no other way to keep moving. Your *why* will give you the stamina to keep pursuing your goals no matter what happens.

Why did you migrate?

Remember to set your career goals as you define why you are moving to a new country. Doing this will provide you clarity along the way, and you will not be distracted by other people's goals.

I have seen many plans and goals being misplaced due to the challenges of migrants settling in a new country. I have seen many of them give up their ambitions and settle for something that they never liked.

So, now is the time to define your goals. If it helps, you may want to discuss them with your significant other (if you have one), a mentor or a close friend. That way, you will have someone who follows your actions and reminds you of your initial intentions.

So, if you haven't done so already, I encourage you to ask yourself why you are here now and what you want out of this new journey in a new land.

We live in a fast-paced world, and you may be distracted if you do not analyse your options and decide on your career. You can easily start chasing someone else's dream, totally neglecting what is important to you. You can also unnecessarily compete with others if you work without a plan and are undecided about your career path.

Planning or goal setting does not have to be elaborate. It can be as simple as coining a simple phrase. Just ensure that you at least have an outline of your plan before you hit the ground running. This will keep you on track, preparing you to confront any challenges that might thwart you.

Challenges do not end. You will face new challenges daily. Moving to a new location does not mean that the challenges are over. You will face new ones. So, brace yourself for new challenges.

Many migrants think their career paths will be perfect, like a straight line right from the onset. But most careers do not start in a perfect manner. They could take the shape of a curve and go all over the place until there is a clear path and direction. If your journey becomes tumultuous, you must stay as motivated and flexible as possible, all the while keeping your goals in sight.

Let us discuss mindset shifts you need to implement in the early stages of your journey as a migrant so as to improve your ability to achieve your goals.

Career Path

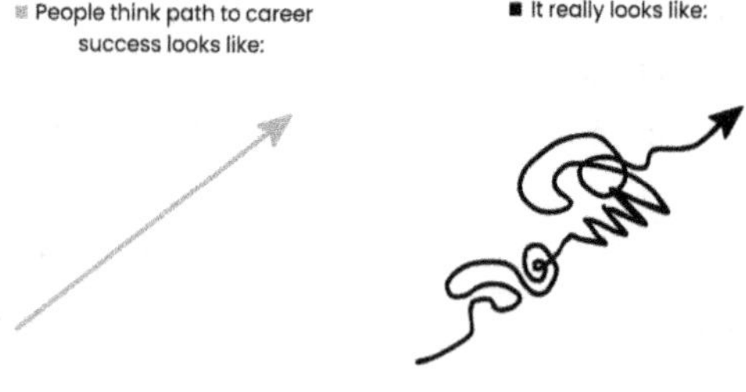

Image inspired by Wendy Terwelp (knocks.com)

Actions:

- Ask yourself why you made this move.
- Know what you want.
- Define your career goals (early).
- Be prepared to face any challenges that come your way.

ADJUSTING THE MINDSET

You will not like this, but I will put it out there anyway.

Leaving your home country is not an achievement.

Leaving your home country for a more developed country is not an achievement. I see many people dreaming about moving to another country. Do not get me wrong, I am happy that your dreams came true but changing your country of residence or relocation is not an achievement by itself. What you make of such a move is the real deal.

I have seen many people move to a new country and become worse than they were back in their home country, and I have also seen professionals become better than they were in their home country. The difference is in the mindset of migrants and how they perceive migration.

My advice to you here is simple.

Refuse to look at migration or relocation as an achievement.

Yes, it may improve the quality of your life because you have access to basic amenities millions of others like you don't have access to, but hey, you must still make the best out of the move and become the best version of yourself in your life.

Successful migrants are the ones who use migration as a

new opportunity to advance their careers and lives. They are the ones who worked hard even in their home country but are more successful in the new countries of their choice because their hard work is now combined with new opportunities, amenities and exposure available to them after migration.

So, do not get me wrong. I am happy you finally moved to your new country, but the journey has not ended yet. There is still work to do. You need to translate your goals, desires, and dreams into something tangible.

You need to use the new land to advance your career and life. You need to first reward yourself by achieving your goals and then give back to the community.

Actions:

- Migration is one of many events that occur in your life. It is not an end.
- You have not yet "arrived". Do not lose focus.
- The challenges that you face in your new country should spur you to perform even better, not underperform.
- Reward yourself by becoming a better you and help others succeed as well.

PLANNING YOUR CAREER

When it comes to career planning, many migrants leave it to chance.

Many become comfortable after landing in their destination country and forget about their original purpose and why they made the move in the first place.

They take care of the other aspects of their lives and leave their careers on autopilot. They allow chance to determine the course of their career journey.

They spend quality time planning the next holiday and the most awesome things they wish to buy.

They plan for the ordinary events.

Do not get me wrong. These activities are great. After all, they are part of our lives.

I believe we should do likewise with our careers.

Why?

The reason is not far-fetched.

Your career is integral to your life, especially as a migrant. An average person spends close to 80,000 hours at work over a lifetime. Essentially, nearly one-third of your life is spent at work.

Shocking, right?

I am just as surprised.

Our careers take up a sizeable chunk of our lives. They are so important that we should take deliberate actions through careful and thorough planning to be the drivers of our careers.

Developing and continually updating a career plan is key to achieving your desired career. A career plan will help you determine the direction you want to take and what you need to do to ensure that you are engaged in meaningful work that meets your career goals.

A career plan does not have to be sophisticated. Think of it as a guiding document that captures your professional field, goals and strategies.

A career plan has three elements:

- You
- Where you are now
- Where you want to be (in X months or years) and how you will achieve this

If you have not been actively planning your career so far, then do it now if you want your efforts in your new country to result in good success.

Now is the best time to act if you do not have a career plan. You do not have to create a 10-page document.

Start by writing out your current employment status, role and where you want to be next the next 6–12 months. Your plan does not have to be perfect. And it can be revised as required over time.

Remember, it is always nice to have a starting point established and agreed upon. You need to evaluate where you are in 6 or 12 months from today.

Do not leave your career on autopilot. It might end up in the ocean.

In Atomic Habits, James Clear says that improving by just 1% is not always noticeable but can be extremely significant in the long term.

The big picture is that if you can become 1% better every day for one year, you will end up 37 times better than at the beginning of the year.

On the other hand, if you become 1% worse every day, you will hit rock bottom by the end of the year. As you can see, making plans and working towards achieving your goals in incremental steps can shape your life.

Only after a year or more will you finally understand the overall value of your good habits and the cost of your bad ones. In the book, Clear gives a notable example of shifting the route of an aeroplane by just a few degrees. He gives the example of flying from Los Angeles to New York City. If the pilot were to make a small adjustment and turn 3.5 degrees south, the plane would end up in Washington, DC, instead of New York City.

As you can see, a small change is barely noticeable when taking off. However, by the end of your journey, you will be hundreds of miles away from your intended destination.

Why this example?

Because small changes that may appear insignificant to you can have big effects on your life if you commit to working towards them daily. You may not see the rewards immediately, but if you stick to your plans and work towards your goals daily, you will reap the rewards in the long term.

UNDERSTANDING YOUR UNIQUENESS

As a migrant, you may fall into the trap of comparing your life and career paths with those of others.

You may be concerned about not matching up with other professionals.

Do not compare your career path and progress with that of others. Comparing your progress with how your friends, colleagues, peers, and other migrants have progressed is not really useful. Our lives and paths are different.

Migration is unique because different and multiple paths are available to different people.

As a migrant, you would have arrived via a specific visa category. You may have met or will meet others who will migrate under a different category.

When I first arrived in Australia in 2016, I was a student. The same week, I saw others arrive on temporary work visas. After getting to know the community, I realised that some others had arrived as permanent residents. We also engaged in different career activities, with each person having unique work and career-related activities.

Why this discussion now?

Your career path will also be different from others' paths. Just as you arrive at various times by different routes, using various paths, your career paths will also differ.

So, understand what works for you and make it your focus area.

You are unique, and so is your career.

There is no need to compare yourself with others.

The only person you are contending against is yourself.

Do not beat yourself too hard.

Aim to improve daily.

These small daily improvements will add up over time.

This should be your approach.

BEWARE OF FREE CAREER ADVICE

When you land in a new country, you will likely meet many good people with good intentions. Everyone will try to help you, offering free advice left, right and centre.

You will probably receive more advice than how often you drink water daily. It is normal.

Everyone tries to help. Sadly, most of the advice is from individuals who have not experienced the same situation but end up giving out free advice to new migrants.

The good news is that you get a lot of information for free. The not-so-good part is that everyone will try to offer free career advice. While their intentions may be good, the information may not be relevant to your situation, and following such advice may hurt your career significantly.

So, your first job will be to analyse the information you receive and decide which will suit you. Do not get me wrong. You can listen to them but you must carefully evaluate the information and decide which one will be right for you.

Let us take John as an example.

John was relocating to a new country to start a new life. He had been waiting for this opportunity for a few years. He was glad that his dream finally came true.

He could now begin to plan the next phase of his career.

One evening, John was on the phone with his friend who had already settled well in his destination country. John sought advice from his friend on how to land a job as quickly as possible.

John's friend advised him to submit 100+ job applications daily.

My heart skipped when I heard this.

Is that even possible?

Thankfully, I was around John and shared my thoughts on why this free advice might not be a good idea. Let me explain why.

Merely sending your resume and applying to several companies will not yield the best results.

Applying for a given role can take several hours. Applying to 100+ jobs every day meant:

- John would apply to all these jobs using one resume.
- John would not have time to customise his resume to suit different jobs.
- John may not even read the job descriptions carefully.

So, the 100+ applications-per-day technique is not effective and practical. These applicants are hardly shortlisted for an interview.

Why?

Their applications are not tailored. Employers spot such applications instantly and rarely shortlist such applicants for an interview.

The result?

The applicants are lengthening their job search journey unknowingly.

This is just one example of free career advice that can go wrong. So, beware as you listen to and follow free career advice, especially from individuals who do not have relevant experience.

Listen but Validate

If you need career advice as a new migrant, I recommend that you speak to career guidance experts and mentors, preferably fellow immigrants who are well-established in their fields.

This group might be able to offer valuable information to assist with your career journey. I also recommend that you speak to more than one professional to obtain different perspectives and check the information before making decisions.

Everyone tries to help, but the advice or solution might not be the best for you. So, it is important to use such information with caution. Among the pieces of advice that you may receive, there will probably be some that are not well suited to you particularly.

Actions:

- Beware of free career advice.
- Everyone tries to help, but unfortunately, not everyone provides helpful information.
- Following bad career advice can severely hurt your career goals.
- Listen, but always validate.

RELAUNCHING YOUR CAREER

You may have come from a professional background or industry that you do not necessarily love or have a passion for. Perhaps you took up a job back in your home country to meet your needs and to improve your family's finances. Maybe jobs were so hard and scarce to come by, and you had to settle for whatever came your way.

The good news is that you can hit a career refresh button after you migrate, depending on your personal circumstances, of course. You can use this opportunity to return to the drawing board to assess what you want from your career.

Let us take Paul's case, for example. Paul was a professional graphics designer in Nigeria before he moved to Canada. That was a job he took up based on availability and urgency. He stayed on the job for a couple of years, and it helped sustain himself and his immediate family. Paul did not like what he was doing but knew that he could not carry on his job for long, and he worked daily on his migration plans.

When Paul finally migrated, he decided not to pursue the same career path but to make a fresh start. Paul had always wanted to work in the Human Resources function. Once Paul arrived in the new country, he immediately enrolled in college and started pursuing a degree in Human Resources. This degree helped him land an HR role in Canada.

Moving to a new country may give you the opportunity you need to kickstart the career that you have always loved. For some though, it could be an opportunity to simply continue from where they had been before migrating to a new country. Think deeply about what you want and stick to it. Remember, no two career paths are the same. So, find out what works for you and decide accordingly.

PREPARING TO FACE CHALLENGES

Migrating to another country can come with fresh challenges, especially new ones that you never knew existed.

You must be ready to take control of your career and deal with any challenges that might come your way. You will experience new challenges 99% of the time, and these are likely to be what you have never faced in your previous location. There is nothing wrong with you. Nothing is wrong with your personality, too. It is just that when you move to a new country, you are bound to face new challenges.

For instance, when Maureen moved to the UK from sub-Saharan Africa, she knew that she would have to face new challenges. As an IT professional in her home country, she was comfortable and stayed in the same job for over five years. When the opportunity to move to a new country presented itself, Maureen believed that she would have no problems adapting to a new country to continue her career and life. Unfortunately, when she arrived in the UK after three months, she understood that adapting quickly to a new country could be quite difficult. She faced several challenges finding suitable roles in her industry.

Moving from a developing country to a developed country will come with its unique challenges. The ways of doing certain things in your home country might be different from how it is done in the new country you are in.

Understanding your role or career as it pertains to the new country you are moving to will help you navigate the initial challenges you might encounter as you settle into your new country.

Understanding Qualification Requirements and Competition

Depending on your role, sector or job, you may find more people available for the jobs you routinely did back home. You may have acquired a degree back home to work in a profession. In the new country, you may find that a formal degree is not required to work in the same field as yours. You may have to compete with more individuals available in that field in your destination country. If you find yourself in this situation, you may have to find other ways of adding new skills to beat the competition; otherwise, you might find yourself struggling to get a job.

Understanding the workplace culture and environment

I remember many years ago, at one of my casual jobs when a colleague asked me if I had gone for "morning tea", I told them I was not interested in having tea at that time. I was told that the phrase meant going for a short break and not necessarily drinking tea. This is one example, but there are many more.

Migrants must make themselves familiar with common idioms. In the workplace, not understanding idioms can lead to confusion and mistakes. Usually, most countries have diverse cultures, languages, and idioms. Not being highly proficient in the local language might affect the ability of migrants to advance in their careers or even to secure employment.

Most people like me are shocked by differences in culture. When I first arrived in Australia, I had to learn new terminologies and new ways of doing things.

Regarding migrants, a major concern of employers will be recruiting the right talent who have cultural understanding. This simply means that whether you understand their workplace culture, operational procedures as well as the primary sources of resources and information. That explains why local companies usually prefer candidates with local work experience. Not being selected does not necessarily mean that you do not have the skills to perform the job. It just means that they want someone who understands how things work in that setting.

As you can see, there might be some challenges as you navigate your career in the new country. The types of challenges you face might also vary depending on your location.

There is no need to worry. You will be fine. Most people tend to adapt well to the new social dynamics after some time. Let us trace the career paths of some migrants.

A MIGRANT'S CAREER PATH

In the introduction, we discussed the basics of getting started and provided some key tips to stay focused on your path.

We will now go over some common career paths that I have noticed among migrants. Your career path will likely be similar to one of these paths, so knowing the types of paths and understanding what to expect while you are on a particular path is crucial for your career success as a new migrant.

As a migrant, you have at least four potential career paths to choose from, namely, the Survival Path, Student Path, Professional Path or Entrepreneur Path. This observation is based on my personal experience as a migrant as well as on the experience of other migrants. There is no right or wrong path, and the earlier you decide what you want to do and stick to your chosen path, the easier it will be to follow it.

Everything you do really depends on what your temperament is, what you want and your current situation.

Let us dive deep into each of these paths to understand them better and determine how you can best navigate them to achieve your career goals.

PART II

THE SURVIVAL PATH

John was a professional engineer back in Africa. He had long dreamed of migrating to Canada with his young family. He planned to relocate to Canada and work in the industry to earn more for himself and give his family the better life that they deserve.

John had just arrived in Canada as a migrant. After three months of settling into the new environment and buying the basic items he needed to set up his new home, he realised that he would soon run out of money. John had to start making money fast to support himself and his family.

This is the dilemma many migrants face after landing in a new country. Many do not realise how expensive their new destination can be and how quickly they must get a job to sustain themselves.

Making money-related decisions

As in the case of John, the early stages of a migrant's life are mostly about survival. Yes, you must survive the new environment, especially financially. Your bank savings will soon become your lifeline, and you will check your account balance multiple times daily to keep yourself in check.

You want to know the extent of your financial situation and whether there is anything to start worrying about. You check how much you have left before committing to anything financially or making a purchase.

Yes, money will probably be one of the most important factors in the decisions you will make as a migrant. There is nothing wrong with that. It is like that for most people, especially if you have migrated from a low- and middle-income country.

As a new migrant, you are more likely to find that the cost of living is significantly higher than that in your home country, and some items you bought, or services you received without paying anything may now cost money. They can be extremely expensive too!

This is why some migrants switch to survival mode quickly.

After three months in Canada, John realised he did not have much wiggle room financially. He had to get just any job to make sure his family did not starve. He had to keep paying his rent and other bills. John started working as a casual staff in a warehouse doing menial tasks to get paid.

Grasping the Reality of Survival

Do not be surprised. This is what most migrants go through. When bills hit, you will have to look for a quick way to support your family in your new country.

Yes, even if you had been a professional back in your home country, like John, who is an engineer, you will quickly learn that finding a job in your original profession on arrival in your new country can be challenging. It is not impossible, but it can be difficult.

Most employers prefer professionals with some local experience and education. Depending on your professional path or industry, you may need to complete certain licensing or other professional registrations, too.

When you add the number of applications, interview stages, and wait times to this, you will see that landing your dream job can take months under normal circumstances. It can take longer, depending on your role and industry and any other requirements you need to fulfil. If you possess a strong network and job-hunting skills, it is possible to land a job before arrival. Of course, such happenings are exceedingly rare. Most migrants look for jobs only on arrival.

The problem is that you do not have much time to wait after arrival. In John's case, he wants to provide his 3-year-old with more than just food and other basic needs.

So, what options does he have?

He must take up any casual job that comes his way. To start working casual jobs, you need little or no training. Usually, a quick certification or training, which may take a day or a couple of weeks, will be enough.

Most migrants initially tend to go this route to start earning money and look after themselves and their family members. They turn to these suboptimal jobs to make a living until they can find some other job that they truly desire.

There are no problems with this at all.

However, I have noticed that most migrants who take up these jobs do not like them and fail to make the best of them. These jobs, despite being casual ones, can be instrumental in your early career. In addition to helping you earn money, these jobs can help you grow your network and gain transferrable skills.

If you ever have to take up survival jobs to keep paying your bills, do not lose heart; it's not the end of the world. That expe-

rience can be one of the most life-changing encounters for a
new migrant.

HOW I BECAME INDISPENSABLE IN A JOB I DISLIKED

When I arrived in Australia in 2016, I realised that I had to take up suboptimal casual jobs, like many other migrants do. I worked in warehousing and other sectors part-time to meet my living expenses.

There is nothing wrong with working suboptimal or low-value jobs to meet immediate needs. These jobs can serve as a stepping stone to understanding work requirements and gaining exposure to the work environment.

Honestly, these casual jobs taught me more life and career lessons than anyone else ever did. You can apply the survival skills, such as adaptability and mental resilience, in everyday life. Below are some steps from my personal experience of which I made the best use.

#1. Giving Your Best Effort at Work

Excellence is key.

Yes, it was not my dream job, but I was being paid in return for services; therefore, obviously, I had to fulfil my part of the bargain by putting in my best efforts in the job.

It was also in my best interest to excel in this job if I wanted to be given the work on an ongoing basis.

The jobs you may consider casual or suboptimal are also competitive. Most companies are ruthless with casual staff and will let them go if they think they are underperforming and not giving their best.

By doing your best, you are at least guaranteed that you will be in the good books of your employer; you will likely be given more or better opportunities. If you underperform, however, you risk losing your job.

#2. Growing a Positive Mindset

No matter what your job or current situation is, approaching it daily with a positive attitude is crucial. Even if you do not like your job, think of ways to make it more enjoyable. You'll be more productive and cheerful at work if you develop a positive attitude.

I maintained a positive attitude regardless of my situation. I was not worried that it was not my dream role. A positive mindset allows you to be your best self and perform well.

I have encountered casual staff who have negative attitudes towards work because they believe that they are better than everyone else. They often disobeyed instructions and did not cooperate with fellow team members. They just assumed that they were too 'big' to be in such a casual job, and this sadly reflected in their behaviour. Of course, they were let go. They lost their source of income, and they had to start looking for work again.

It is not always easy to stay motivated and happy in a role you consider does not match your skillsets. Everybody has a bad day sometimes. However, by trying to be optimistic, you can wade through any challenge and make the most of your situation.

#3. Learning from Experiences

Every situation or challenge in life has something positive to offer.

The truth is that we tend to focus more on negative experiences than on positive ones. Focusing on negative experiences will cloud your judgements. When you focus on the negative experiences and outcomes, you indirectly shut your mindset towards accepting opportunities and learning new things.

No one likes doing work that they are not passionate about, but it doesn't mean that you can't learn to do it well.

Working at a job that you do not love will be challenging for the first few weeks or months. In fact, you might start regretting your decision to move to a new country. I felt that way, too, and many migrants like you feel that way as well. I had a friend who often cried when he had to resume his casual job at 5 a.m. He had not imagined earlier that he would need to go through this challenge to support himself and his family.

Remain committed and determined to learn from your experiences and be ready with an open mind to learn even in roles that do not require your professional skills. These opportunities have plenty to offer if you remain positive and choose to learn from them.

Remember, no experience is wasted.

#4. Staying Humble and Calm

Everyone has something to offer, and everyone deserves to be respected.

Even if you are working at a job that you do not like, you must be professional and respectful to your colleagues and refuse to let this low point in your life reflect in your behaviour.

This was particularly challenging for me as a postgraduate student at a top University in Australia. I could not understand why I had to do an odd job to get by. I thought I deserved better since I had academic degrees to land jobs that aligned with my skills.

I tried as much as I could to find the good in the unskilled job and my colleagues. In the end, I realised everyone has something unique to offer. I learned a great deal by staying humble, teachable and respectful of my colleagues.

If you remain calm, you will find that there is much to learn, even from those colleagues who you consider are not at the same level as you in your career. Remember that we are all just humans trying to do our best. No one is perfect, and everyone deserves respect.

#5. Working Towards the End Goal

Waking up every day and turning up for a job that you do not like can be depressing. You probably lose motivation on some days, as I did. One way that was helpful to me was to have a goal and work towards it daily.

Despite working in an undesirable job, I spent time developing my skills for my dream role, networking and speaking to other professionals in my fields of interest.

A colleague we worked with in this role together came across my LinkedIn profile and rang my phone asking if I truly had the skills listed on my LinkedIn profile.

He did not believe I could have time to gain these skills while working in an undesirable work environment. He did not imagine I had other plans and means to achieve my goals.

Remember, your current state does not define you. Work towards your desired goals daily. Contribute your 1%, which will pay off over time like compound interest.

#6. Cultivating an Interest in Your Job

Working in a job you do not like can be challenging, but if you want to give your best, it is essential that you are genuinely interested in the role. You want to be able to give your best on the job to be retained.

You may think you are safe if you are doing the bare minimum at your job.

But not caring about your work is one of the quickest ways to be let go from the job.

Employers pay money in exchange for your services, so you must fulfil your part by putting in your best. Be passionate and interested in your work, even if you do not love it.

By putting in extra effort and being a team player, you'll make yourself invaluable to the organisation and learn from others. Your mindset begins to change over time, and you will begin to love the role. And who knows — maybe eventually, you will find something more exciting and land your dream role within your current company. We will discuss this later.

#7. Unwinding and Self-Caring

A fantastic way to unwind and forget my current struggles was taking breaks and doing the things I love outside of my undesired job.

I often visited friends and people that mattered to me. I flew to neighbouring states and cities to explore the places that I love.

Life gets busy, as does work, particularly jobs you consider less desired. Therefore, looking after your physical and mental health is essential.

Take breaks when possible.

Converting Adversities into Opportunities

Those years working jobs I did not desire turned out to be some of the most critical moments of my life.

Not because I particularly enjoyed the boring, low-level job but because of who I had become while working these jobs.

Here are some potential benefits if you stick your head up high in these low moments.

Excellence leads to growth

While working these jobs, I realised that strong performers were given higher responsibilities, which often meant cooler casual roles.

You will start to gain recognition and be rewarded with more growth opportunities when you give your best in a job despite not liking it.

We would sometimes look at some of these colleagues in awe and amazement and wonder why the managers would trust them with such a level of responsibility.

Again, the secret is to do excellent work, put in your best, show initiative and build trust.

Setting the Bar High

You become the gold standard when you become good at your job.

You can set standards for a job you hate.

You heard me right.

A colleague was contacted about four months after he took a short break to focus on other priorities. The organisation needed someone for an urgent cover.

After arriving at the job that day, he realised they were

heavily short-staffed. He knew staffing was not the problem as the agency responsible had enough staffing to keep the role going.

He then went to ask the manager why they had not hired replacement staff. The manager told him something along the lines of:

"We have had issues finding the right person since you left this role. It is not their fault; we got so used to you after you set such high standards that everyone else who came afterwards struggled to live up to".

You become a standard when you become good at jobs by being genuinely interested in the position and those around you.

Again, it is not about you. It is about the person you become with this new approach to work.

Giving your all at work will help set new standards for yourself and others. Not to mention, an outstanding performance will make you feel good about yourself. So, give it your all, even if you do not love your unskilled job.

Learning Transferable Skills

No experience is ever lost.

Despite working these odd jobs, I was patient to make the best of it by learning as much as possible.

I was in an entirely new country and realised any lesson was good. I was ready to learn and gain transferable skills to adapt to contemporary society.

Transferable skills are skillsets that can be utilised and transferred across many jobs. You will not stop needing communication, teamwork, leadership, and time management skills. They will always come in handy and follow you wherever you go.

Remember, working a low-level casual job to temporarily

sustain yourself and your family is not the end of the world. This is a common, quick path and should not make you feel less human. Some migrants go through this initial phase to get started and hit the ground running until they are able to find better job opportunities.

It is not about the job. It is about the person you become in the process.

And, of course, it's just a temporary phase in your life, so keep your head up and keep moving. Show value by putting in your best and focusing on making the best out of it.

EXPLOITING AVAILABLE OPPORTUNITIES

Who says you must remain casual at the same company for an extended period?

Sometimes, these casual roles can lead to better opportunities within the same company.

I wish more professional migrants working unskilled casual roles knew and explored this path, as it offers more opportunities without much stress if you strategically plan your job search.

This approach is also excellent because you are already in the organisation. You already have your foot in the door!

A friend used this approach to land a dream role in their current company. They started as casual employees but went on to work in their professional roles within the same company.

We will call him Andy.

Andy is a professional migrant with a background in occupational health and safety.

He was quite intelligent, soft-spoken and confident.

He approached problems positively and thought out of the box to solve challenges.

Andy decided to take up an unskilled role working in a warehouse when he could not find a job in his professional field.

He was about 5ft 10 inches tall and of an average build and was hired to stack boxes of weight up to 15kg in a warehouse in town. The time was one of busy periods around the end of the financial year, and he was kept busy.

When Andy started working at the warehouse, he met other workers sent from the same recruitment agency to the warehouse on a three-month contract. Andy was dedicated and committed to his job.

He was punctual, open to learning, and sought opportunities to grow even though this was not his dream job. He focused on adding value in this role and ensured his employers and contractors had confidence in him.

Four weeks into the role, Andy, an Occupational Health and Safety professional, realised some health and safety gaps in the firm and decided to chat with the manager. Andy expressed his desire to provide advice to ensure that the firm maintained the industry standards.

Andy immediately highlighted some gaps to the manager, demonstrating how the firm could improve its health and safety processes.

The manager shared these points with a senior colleague, who accepted that Andy could provide occupational health and safety advice. Andy was asked to spend 1–2 days per week working specifically on health and safety-related projects in the warehouse and the other days working as a regular warehouse assistant alongside his colleagues.

Andy continued to add value in both roles, and the manager was impressed with how Andy had reshaped the health and safety procedures of the firm. At the end of the three-month contract, Andy's contract was extended for six months, specifically working on health and safety projects, as the firm was looking to improve its processes further.

Unfortunately, Andy's colleagues, who had started at the same time as Andy, were let go since their main project had ended. Andy had also started looking for a permanent full-time role for job security. While Andy worked at the firm, he would update his resume accordingly with the new responsibilities and experience. Andy started getting noticed by other employers after a few weeks.

After two interviews, Andy received a permanent full-time bumper offer with a choice firm. Andy's manager at the warehouse was instrumental in helping Andy land this role, as he provided a great reference to support Andy's application.

Andy's case is one of sheer determination, a positive attitude, and a willingness to have a successful career no matter the work environment. He found opportunities in every situation. He put in his best and was always focused on the positive side. He recognised opportunities and volunteered to add value.

As you can see, there is nothing wrong with working suboptimal or low-value jobs to meet one's needs. However, it may be detrimental not to have an end goal with SMART objectives to achieve it.

Here are some pointers if you wish to use this technique to transition from an unskilled to a more desirable role in your current organisation.

Plan the jobs and the companies

This might seem weird or counterproductive for individuals with urgent financial needs. However, where practicable, it is always a good idea to take up casual or part-time positions in organisations or companies where your professional skills can put you in the limelight. If you are an Engineer, opt for such jobs in an organisation or company in the engineering department. The benefit of this is that you will not only understand the business area but can also add value indirectly while engaging in your casual, less-desired role.

Choose an organisation that supports growth within the organisation

Since your goal is to transition from a less-desired role into a more desired one, you must choose an organisation that promotes growth and transition within the organisation.

Glance through the career page of the company's website to see if you find ads for other roles, as well as casual positions. This is a good sign that they openly post vacancies on their websites, allowing potential candidates to apply directly.

Looking up some of the current and previous staff on professional networks such as LinkedIn to understand their career journey can also be useful. Contacting former or current staff members to learn about their career journeys and potential growth opportunities within the firm is also a good idea.

Attend the interview as if you were being considered for your dream position

Appear confident at the interview and speak like a true professional, but focus on the interview for the role you are being interviewed for (do not get carried away). Do not approach the interview as though it is not important since it is not your dream role. Prepare as much as though you are getting interviewed for your dream role. Read about the business area, the business sector, and your role while highlighting your key strengths. You want to ace the interview and get your foot in the door.

Ask the hiring manager on interview day about the growth potential

During the interview process in many organisations, many questions border around career growth, career plans, and opportunities for improvement. Use this opportunity to let the panel know your long-term career aspirations; however, be careful not to make this your focus or dwell too much on this discussion, as you do not want this to be the highlight of the interview. Ensure that the role you have applied for remains the focus so you can be offered the job. Remember, this is what you ultimately want so that you get your foot in the door before unleashing any other career plans you may have.

Stay connected with the hiring manager

Your chat with the hiring panel does not have to end on the interview day. Ensure you progress these discussions by keeping in touch with the hiring manager or the panel member who looked most excited about your expertise and your willingness to add value from the interview day. Often, this person can be your career evangelist and can introduce you to key contacts. Regularly check in with this person every couple of weeks to chat about the dynamics and your vision within the organisation.

Don't be a "regular"

Anything worth doing at all is worth doing well. You may not love your current unskilled role, but you need to get a good job to be noticed. This is the absolute minimum requirement. You need to put in your best.

Be that individual who puts his hands up to take up ad-hoc responsibilities or tasks when they come up. Show the managers you are dependable and complete tasks as soon as possible while delivering quality work. Doing this will instil confidence in you from the managers, and you will begin to gain recognition.

While working in this role, you want to show your worth as much as possible. Study as much as possible to learn about the job and the business. Contribute as much as you can during team meetings. Be the person who volunteers to take on irregular or out-of-scope tasks that come up. Such initiatives will show your willingness and eagerness to help the team and your responsibility and ownership culture. Think out of the box and suggest ideas to the team. It is not likely that all your ideas will be implemented. Even if only a few of your ideas are accepted and implemented, you will be recognised for doing a good job. Make good suggestions to the managers, ask intelligent questions and let them know you can assist in other roles. Another benefit is that you begin to learn something new, and you may be another team member in your chosen department.

Following industry news and trends.

As you wish to transition from a current role to a more desired "dream role" within the organisation, keeping abreast of the latest events in the business and your dream role is a good idea. Speak to colleagues in those roles and attempt to understand their current challenges. Think about these challenges at the end of the day when you have some free time, brainstorm and design solutions you think may be helpful, and proffer these to the team. You want to ensure this is captured as much as possible via email. Opportunities such as this help you get noticed and gain visibility in the organisation, which you ultimately need.

Another benefit of this approach is that it helps develop your mindset and problem-solving approach as if you were already working in the role you desire. The manager at your choice department may approach you if they need an additional team member. This will be a win for all, as the HR or hiring manager will be happy that they do not have to go through the normal hiring process of advertisement, shortlisting, and interviewing, and you would not have other applicants to contend with. You may just be the one and only candidate to be interviewed for this role!

Engaging with other employees

If you have been provided access to the organisation's intranet and apps, it is a good idea to engage with other staff on social apps like Viva Engage and Workplace. These applications are designed specifically for the organisation and its staff to engage internally. Internal positions are often advertised on these internal networks. If you follow managers in your areas of interest, their posts will appear in your feeds. Do not feel intimidated by your current position. Connect with your teammates on the social network application set up by your organisation. I recommend checking this page daily. Engage in discussions, join groups that interest you, and share ideas with co-workers.

Applying for roles of your choice

Now that you have contributed positively to your current role and shown that you can readily take up new and more challenging responsibilities, it's a good time to start applying for your choice positions as they come up. Remember to keep getting your job done, regardless. Do not assume that you will be automatically considered for the new role. You still must do your part by updating your resume accordingly. Remember to include a cover letter and highlight your skills, achievements and contributions to the organisation.

If you have made a good impression early, having your manager be your reference will not be challenging. Do not assume this will be automatic; you still must speak to them, letting them know about your intentions to apply for an internal role and requesting that you enlist them as your reference. Remember to follow the application guidelines and other requirements specified in the position description, as you might be penalised and lose out entirely if you do not follow these instructions.

Occasionally, you might not find any role that suits you online. If this is the case, you can use your interactions with key staff to suggest new ideas and express your desire to work in your dream role. You can also choose to volunteer in your choice department for a couple of hours per week.

By following this simple technique in 2019, I was able to secure my dream job within the same organisation where I worked as a casual staff member. I, however, did not take up the role and left the organisation because another organisation had offered me an opportunity I preferred.

Remember, do not settle for an unskilled role that you do not love if you have the passion to work in the role of your choice. Let your organisation know what you stand for and what you want. You have already got your leg in the door, and chances are they will listen to you and see how they can help you.

Keeping Your Manager Informed

Your manager will most likely become aware of intentions and networking moves, so letting them know before applying for the position or after applying is a good idea.

You do not want your manager to hear from another source. More importantly, most internal jobs require that current managers sign off to let you go. If you want to execute this process without your manager, it is not a good idea, as you would not leave a good impression.

You might also lose your manager's trust in the process. Let your manager know that you are applying to hone your skills, gain additional skills, take on more challenging work, etc. Be honest about your reasons and ensure you do not tarnish your current position or speak low of your colleagues. Ensure your manager gains your trust; he is your best internal reference.

Acing the Interview

Do not assume you will not be interviewed for this role because you are an internal candidate already familiar with the team and the organisation. Treat this interview or opportunity as though you were applying from the outside.

Prepare for the interview and be prepared to confidently answer questions and communicate your value.

PURSUING CAREER GOALS

Life can get rough while working in these casual, unskilled roles, and you might soon find yourself unfulfilled and unhappy with no progress in your career. Here are a few pointers to help you pursue your desired career goals.

Investing in Your Career Savings Account

Always Pay Yourself, no matter what

Working in a low casual job can mean you will return home at the end of each day tired, exhausted, demotivated and unhappy with your life and career.

There is nothing wrong with this feeling. It is normal.

I often returned home tired most days. Nevertheless, I spent some hours investing in my career savings account.

How?

- By reaching out to a new network
- Applying for jobs

- Reading a book
- Publishing an article

I soon learned that these activities gave me the necessary boost to keep going. It is like an investment in my future career savings account.

Even if my day was terrible, I invested time in my career savings account. It was a simple trick that kept me going and looking forward to the future.

When things are rough, losing focus on yourself or your future goals is easy.

Your current state is not what you want, which might make you occasionally sad.

This state might be while engaging in a low-skilled job or a job you do not like.

No matter what, do not leave your career savings account empty.

Do something toward your goal daily.

Ensure you spend some time working for your future self. Do something that adds up to the future you dream of.

These minor actions will add up over time. They will become significant, and you will be happy you did.

Ultimately, the little time I spent contributing tiny bits to my career savings account paid off.

Remember Andy, the Health and Safety professional who transition from a casual to a professional role in his current organisation? He invested in his career savings account daily by staying relevant and seeking opportunities that would help him add value. He also applied for other roles while working at the warehouse. He leveraged his work experience as a health and safety professional to land another role with bumper pay in another organisation.

Your career Is like an investment bank account. What you

deposit compounds over time and yields results based on your level of savings.

Keep it running by contributing significant learning and development activities to this account regardless of your current situation.

Leaving your career savings account unattended might result in little or no yield when you are ready to harvest.

Contribute your 1% daily. In the long run, it will add up.

Quitting Unsuitable Jobs

When Adam arrived in Australia as a migrant and started his casual job to sustain himself and his young family Immediately, he thought he would be just for the short term. He did not realise he would spend over seven years of his life doing the job he hated and eventually getting stuck in a role he picked up temporarily so he could work while he reshaped his engineering career.

Adam's case is not uncommon in many destination countries. Like Adam, migrants land casual suboptimal roles in the country to get up and running, only to find themselves stuck in it for years and unable to revert to their original profession.

Yes, it happens regularly, and I see it often.

Jobs that you do not love can come in handy when you are fresh in a country and need to get up and running as soon as possible. Yes, you need the money to keep your body and soul together, but it does not have to be a job you get stuck on and spend nearly the rest of your life doing.

These casual suboptimal or menial jobs can quickly replace your professional life, and it might be hard to go back to your original career.

And if you have been doing these causal jobs for long, it can be difficult to return to your original profession. This creates a huge gap in your resume and professional profile, making it harder for you to switch.

Ultimately, you accept your fate and the life your new journey has thrown at you and cruise to retirement.

Of course, some migrants do not mind this lifestyle, but if you do, then you can take and should take bold moves and rewrite your story.

Sure, jobs are jobs; after all, you need the money from it, right? But I tell you: There's fulfilment in doing what you love. There is the fulfilling part of it that gives you complete satisfaction.

"But I make money", Sam said.

When Sam shared his opinion about this subject, he told me it was completely okay to do what you do not love and ultimately make money to fulfil your needs.

I agree with him. And ultimately, this depends on your goals and vision. If you desire career fulfilment, I highly recommend you do not get stuck in your career doing what you don't love, where you spend the better part of your day hating yourself and wishing you were not doing the job you hate.

Ask yourself: if money were not part of the equation and you had the opportunity to do anything else, would you still be doing what you are doing now? You should find fulfilment in whatever you do. Doing it makes you feel complete and opens up further opportunities as you grow in your career.

While you may be making money, it does not resolve your career fulfilment needs. It does not give you the freedom and choice to do what you want to do.

Do not get me wrong, you can do what you love and make money too. So why do what you do not like for the rest of your life because of money? If I were you, I would do what I love and make money. You can have both, and that should be your goal.

The message is clear: if you possess a professional background, unskilled and suboptimal jobs should be taken up at critical points when you need a little push, like jumpstarting your career, finances, and stability. They should not replace your whole life and vision for your career. It is like kickstarting your car battery after it has gone flat. If your battery is flat, you get help for kickstarting it, but that does not mean you should not make plans for a replacement as soon as possible. Failing to do that can leave you stuck anytime when on lonely motorways.

Jump-start your career when you need to and do whatever (legally allowed) comes your way for survival, but it should not replace your ultimate vision and life. It is beyond money; it is about finding fulfilment and loving what you do to make a difference. You can have both career fulfilment and money.

Earning money as a casual employee

After Joe arrived and settled in the UK as a new migrant, he immediately realised the opportunity to work on a casual basis and support himself and his family while he organises his tech profession. When you move to a new country with high living expenses, you must immediately start working to meet your living expenses.

Five years on, Joe still works at the same unskilled jobs he worked when he first arrived in the country. When I chatted with Joe, he told me he was happy combining multiple jobs and earning more than his friends who work full-time in corporate organisations.

Joe told me he earned 3,000 pounds per month combining 2–3 jobs on a casual basis. He told me that he worked 300 hours per month to make this money. He also told me his friends who work in corporate jobs do not make more than 2,000 pounds monthly, and he was happy with his take-home pay.

But Joe's argument was illogical. I will explain in a moment.

While it appears as though Joe makes a lot of money, his

hourly rate is low because he put in many work hours. It would have been better if he worked less time and used his free time to pursue his main career goals.

A 3,000-pound income for 300 hours per month is approximately 10 pounds per hour. This was what Joe earned. On the other hand, his friends who work 150 hours per month and take home 2,000 pounds receive a slightly greater amount (13.3 pounds per hour). While it seems as if Joe makes more money than his friends when you consider the monthly income, you find that he actually earns less than what his friends earn when you compare the hourly rates.

Joe looks at the absolute income. When you look at the absolute income, you consider only your net or gross income without considering how much time and effort you put in to make such money.

Relative vs. Absolute Income

In his *Four-Hour Workweek*, Tim Ferris discusses the difference between relative and absolute income.

Relative income is more important than absolute income. Relative income looks at money and time, whereas absolute income only looks at money. The former method is how you should assess your income and career.

Focus on "relative income" instead of "absolute income". Relative income can be increased by increasing total income for the same hours, getting the same income for fewer hours, or some combination thereof. More options with more life.

Returning to Joe's story, he could potentially be making more money in the longer term if he devoted his time and effort outside of work to relaunch his IT career. His net worth is beyond the amount of money he makes from multiple jobs, but the amount of time he saves, as well as the free time he has to pursue other important career goals which can potentially help him earn more.

The lesson here is that being tempted by the total amount of money you make by putting in multiple hours across multiple jobs is easy. This is not sustainable in the long term. You want to be able to work just as much and have a life outside of work to spend time with your loved ones. This is how you achieve both financial rewards and build your career capital.

Of course, you can make this a marathon to fulfil some urgent financial responsibilities over the short term, but this shouldn't take over your life and career. Beyond working round the clock daily, you also need an excellent quality of life.

Ultimately, you want balance, which comes from your ability to have enough time to pursue your career goals instead of getting stuck working multiple unskilled jobs with no time for your main or original career, life and family.

Preparing to lose some to win some

In 2019, I also worked at multiple jobs. I wanted to use the funding to support my family for an urgent need. I did this for a couple of months, and it worked well. However, once I started a 9–5 in a consulting firm, it became difficult for me to take up any extra jobs and earn more money.

When I got my first full-time job, it was as if I had been robbed. My total income was reduced by half. I just could not believe it. Then I began asking myself: is it worth finding a career in consulting or keep working across multiple casual jobs?

You may find this interesting, but it is not as easy as it appears to be. It is hard when you lose an income that you have become used to, and so have to change the lifestyle you have become adapted to.

Anyway, I decided there was no going back and had to stick

to my new routine. However, while working 9–5, I would pick up random extra jobs on weekends. I soon realised that the income from these extra jobs hurt me more than they benefited me. I earned extra money occasionally but spent so much time away from home that I became unhappy. I also could not continue my learning and development plans to be at my best in my full-time job. Because each time I came up with a learning goal, I did not achieve it because I was busy working extra hours elsewhere over the weekend.

Ultimately, I decided to stop all weekend work to learn and develop skills that would help me in my full-time role.

Once I stopped taking up extra weekend work, I spent my weekends focussing on my goals and development plans. Although I lost nearly a part of my income by giving up the extra work, it was the best decision I have made for myself yet.

The relative income was much better than the absolute income. I now had plenty of free time and used it to pursue learning and development activities that helped develop my skills. After a couple of months, I applied for better-paying roles. In the end, it paid off. I was able to land better jobs with more pay using the new skills that I acquired using my free time. Soon, I could earn just as much working on a full-time job at 40 hours per week as working two full-time jobs at 80 hours per week.

Imagine that I continued working all weekends, lacked time, and could not develop my skills. Chances are, I would have probably been doing that. I might have still been on a low-pay job, with no real career success, promotions, or progress, had I not decided to focus and stick with it.

Identifying the Trade-offs

Jake has a big family. His day job alone would not pay all his bills. Jake works in health care during the day and picks up more casual jobs at nights and weekends. I have not seen Jake in about a year. Each time we spoke on the phone, he told me he spends so much time working that he barely has time with his family. His kids are 6 and 4 years old. The kids are growing up fast, and he is not spending much time with them. He told me he spends more time working to pay their tuition fees to give the best. He works 80 hours per week. The education of his children is no doubt important. My question is, for how long more does he have to work so hard to look after his family? Jake has a decision to make around finding new ways to cater for his young family without overworking and spending so much time away from him.

Sometimes, you must lose some to win some. You have to take a hit to prepare a foundation for the future you want.

If you want to unleash your true potential and be at your best, you must be ready to put in more time and effort to pursue the life you want. You will need to look beyond spending a ridiculous amount of time working to have more money in reserve. You must begin to think about earning just as much by putting in minimal effort so you can spend most of your time with those that matter to you. You want a balanced and rewarding life that allows you to live the life you want. You want to work to live and not live to work.

In the early stages, you can decide to put in more hours at work to meet a specific goal, but you should also agree on an upper limit and focus more on increasing your relative income and forgo absolute income.

Working at multiple jobs

There are several reasons why you should not work more hours to earn more money. The truth is that while the immediate income and paycheck can be short-term rewarding, it can pose a significant risk to your health, well-being, family, and social life.

Working more hours than usual means spending more time away from your family. The family, which you value the most, will spend less time with you at home, which might also cause the bond to get used to the fact that you are not always home and deprive them of your presence.

This can also mean more time away from your social circle, which might impact your relationships with the most important people.

Most casual jobs, as they are called, are not mostly related to your professional fields. You may not be able to add these work episodes to your professional resume. Therefore, devoting more time for these jobs can cause significant gaps in your resume, which might make it harder for you to find work in your original or main profession.

So, take care before replacing your main career with menial or casual jobs for extended periods. While the financial rewards are great, they can cause long-term side effects on your career and social and mental wellbeing.

Again, I am not opposed to you putting in a great deal of work to look after yourself and your loved ones. I only emphasise that you must remember that you have a long-term goal and that working round the clock is not sustainable. Aside from the impacts on your family, loved ones and your profession, it can also lead to burnout as you might not have sufficient time to rest and unwind after prolonged work hours.

Working casual jobs and moving from one shift job to another can be convenient. However, this can be mentally unstimulating and unfulfilling in the long term and cause a lack of growth.

Remember to have an exit strategy if you decide to go this route temporarily. Not having a career plan or goal can mean that you travel on this path for a longer period than you originally intended. This might have an unfulfilling effect on your life, family, and career.

Your goal is to keep your work hours to the minimum with increasing income to give you the balance you need in other areas of your life. Time will pass quickly, and you will forever wonder what you did with your life and career.

Ultimately, survival jobs can help you kickstart life as a new migrant, provide a source of income and serve as an opportunity to gain exposure and transferable skills. You want to make this path as short as possible. The path to survival should not become the primary path in your career at any point in time.

Don't tie your income to your time

The last thing you want to do is to tie your income to your time (see image below). In this case, your income only grows when you take up more work hours or work multiple casual jobs. While this approach might appeal to many migrants, it is not sustainable for long periods.

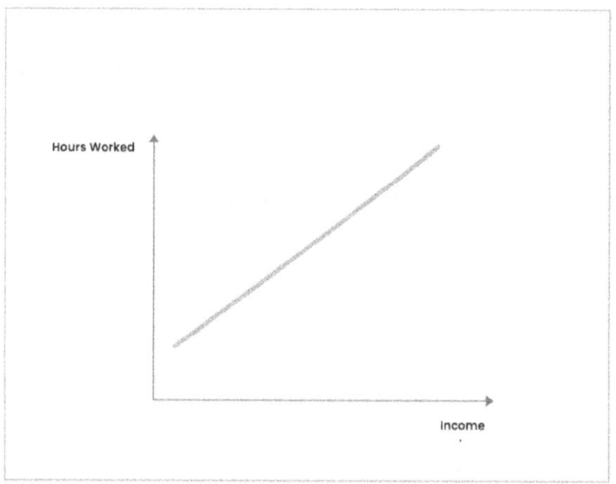

Fig: Income vs work hours

If you have to spend time for every cent you make, then you

will soon run out of hours because time is limited. You cannot have more than 24 hours per day. No one does.

When this happens, you are stuck at a fixed income because you no longer have any available hours to work. Assuming you earn $20 an hour, the maximum you can earn working for 24 hours straight is $480 or $3,360 over seven days, assuming you work round the clock, which is almost impossible.

Your income might look good, but you might soon find it challenging once your needs grow yet again and you need more money. At this stage, you do not have any more free hours to work.

Your best bet is to ensure you are growing your career so that your income grows while you do not work extra hours. It is possible to boost your income while your work hours stay the same. If this is what you want, be prepared to hold back some hours to develop yourself and your skills daily.

In the next session, we will discuss your options if you choose to return to school as a new migrant.

Actions:

- Find survival jobs to keep you financially healthy if you need to
- Stay positive with an open mindset and learn as much as possible.
- Keep your focus on your main or original career and work towards it daily

PART III

———

THE STUDENT PATH

Some migrants also explore the option to return to school to obtain a local qualification or degree.

Darsh had just arrived in the UK from India.

Back home, he worked at a bank and had a bachelor's degree in commerce and an MBA. He was doing fine back home as he had the requirements to land a banking job.

When the thought of moving to the UK with his family first came to mind, he did not understand how to navigate his early career once he arrived in the UK. After speaking to one or two friends, he started his career again by returning to school. Once he arrived in the UK, he hit the ground running by enrolling in another degree in accounting.

No problems with that.

The Student Path is one of the most favoured paths for some migrants. It can be a quick way to gain new skills and restart your career. It is also a good avenue to entrench yourself in society, provided you have the money.

While this path offers a quick way to get started, it can be quite expensive.

For other professionals, the thought of returning to the classroom, taking assignments and attending lectures while looking after oneself and family is also high. These professionals do not want this route, especially if they have achieved multiple degrees.

As a new migrant, one option that will potentially appeal to you is returning to school to get a degree. This option becomes more obvious if your previous education or degree was from low- and middle-income countries and you worked in these countries before migrating.

Some employers tend to favour those with local education, so many consider these options viable. While returning to school may sound like a great idea, it comes with many responsibilities worth considering before enrolling.

John, who had just completed his second master's degree, contacted me and considered enrolling in another degree.

He has had difficulties landing jobs, so he thought an additional degree may boost his chances of landing the desired role. He was happy to enrol again as a student for another year or two to obtain this degree.

Like Darsh, John's story is not unfamiliar to me.

I have met with young professionals considering returning to school for another degree. After unsuccessful attempts to land their dream role in the industry, many consider this move. They believe that an additional degree will break the unemployment chain.

Education is not cheap. The cost keeps going up every year with rising inflation.

Depending on where you are and your options, you will be looking at tens of thousands of dollars. Not only that, but you would also need to be a student for one or two years to obtain your degree. Full-time academics will fully occupy your time.

But wait?

What next after John's third degree?

What if he doesn't get a job after this degree?

Would he enrol in the fourth one? I am not sure this will be a good idea. He might have too many degrees for his portfolio without practical work experience.

If you find yourself in a similar situation, there are a few things to consider before taking such decisions.

Reconsidering enrolling

Going to school or enrolling in another degree program is good. I encourage those I meet to get an education. However, there may be a point when it may not necessarily add much value.

If you already have two or three postgraduate degrees and are not finding roles, re-thinking your decision to enrol in another degree may be worth considering.

Pause and re-assess whether that new degree will help you land your dream job. Pausing and giving it fresh thought may help you make a more informed decision.

Consulting Professionals in Your Field

Sometimes, we are not the best decision-makers for ourselves. Therefore, it may also be helpful to speak to professionals around you.

Go on LinkedIn and find individuals working in your dream roles. Speak to them about your new study plans and ask whether another degree will help you get your desired role.

In most cases, you do not need to cough out tens of thousands of dollars to find a job. Speaking to people may open your mindset and help you discover your needs.

Revising Your Strategy

After graduating, I tried applying for jobs online but was not successful. No matter how I tried, it did not work out.

One day, I stopped everything I did as they yielded zero results. I stopped because I knew they were not working. I knew there had to be a better strategy.

After a few weeks, I started getting traction. In the end, I landed multiple roles in my field.

If you are job hunting without success, sometimes, all you need to do is to revisit your strategy.

Evaluate your job search results and change your strategies if they are not yielding results. For example, consider using offline approaches if your online methods are not working.

Changing your strategy may solve your job hunting, but not necessarily a new $50,000+ degree.

Re-Assessing Your Strengths

Brand-new academic degrees are low-hanging fruits.

They are easily accessible when you can afford the tuition fees. That you find it easy to enrol for new degrees does not mean it will solve your job search problems.

Job searching requires a strategy. You must understand your strengths and interests. You must understand who you are to find these roles in the job market.

If you struggle to land a job after multiple degrees, consider re-assessing your strengths and interests to understand your wants. This step may solve your challenges instead of another university degree.

While the Student Path is quick, you can easily find yourself going to school after school without real progress. You find yourself completing one degree after the other. Not necessarily because you need them but because they are available to you as a low-hanging fruit. This becomes common and attractive when you can access some student loans, making you think you can keep going.

As general advice, if you think you need to complete degrees without a specific need, you are probably doing it wrong. You may need to change your strategy and solve your real career challenges. Avoid this degree loop.

In most developed countries, having multiple degrees does not improve your chances of landing a role unless, of course, you are changing fields completely.

An additional degree may not necessarily be the solution to your job-hunting woes.

Before enrolling in a new degree (especially after you already have 2–3 degrees), re-assess your situation by considering whether you need that extra degree.

Take it further by speaking to professionals in your field on LinkedIn to hear their views on whether you need that degree for the roles you want.

In addition, re-assess your strengths and change your job search strategy if you find out it's not producing results.

The solution to your job search challenges might be cheaper than you think.

GET GOING FIRST

Your goal is to get settled and start working as soon as possible.

While returning to school may sound like a great idea, your main goal is to settle and earn an income, especially when you have a family and move with other dependents. The cost of living can be expensive, so you therefore want to have some time to make a living for yourself and your family.

My advice to you, even if you decide to return to school, is to find work as soon as possible to keep you going. Ultimately, you need money to survive and pay your bills, and time waits for no one.

You might not find a perfect job for a start, but you can get going with your current job and keep looking for your dream role in the industry. You will gain more clarity on what to do next.

Applying for Student loans or Grants

After evaluating all options, if you decide to return to school, you may want to apply for grants or loans. Some destination countries like Canada and Australia, for example, make quick student loans or grant schemes by which the government funds the education of migrant students. This may be a good alternative, especially if you do not want to put a hole in your pocket.

Aside from this funding, you may also want to check out the scholarship opportunities available to domestic students. Some scholarships are available to domestic students. You might be lucky to win one of them.

When Lima arrived in Australia and while settling and preparing to go back to Uni to earn a postgraduate degree, she realised the government had just launched a new funding initiative to help provide up to 70% funding to individuals wanting to take up short courses within certain sectors. This was part of the government initiative to bridge the education gap and encourage professionals to take college courses. In Lima's case, this was a great opportunity for her. She was able to take up the grant and paid a gap to obtain her degree.

So, check carefully what might be offered to you if you are keen to return to the classroom before paying full fees out of pocket from your limited savings.

Completing short courses and top up degrees

If you decide to enrol for a degree, it may be worth checking out short courses such as graduate certificate and diploma courses. These are short and are offered across both colleges and universities. Sometimes, you only need a quick course that brings you exposure and connection and teaches you about the country's culture.

Short courses are always a great idea if you do not wish to spend over 12 months or close to 2 years in the university and then start all over again. They can serve as a break-even point for you to relaunch your career by gaining a local education and looking for the work you want.

If you are already working too, you may complete a shorter course than if the courses were long.

When Adam migrated to Australia, he wanted a master's degree. However, once he enrolled in the University, he realised a graduate certificate might work for what he intended, so he broke his study plans into three.

He would first need to complete a certificate program, which would take nearly 3–6 months (one semester long), then the option to continue with a diploma which would take another six months. After completing his diploma, he would have the opportunity to progress to a master's degree, which would take one year (two semesters) after the diploma.

It turned out Adam never returned to the University after completing a graduate certificate for one semester. He realised the graduate certificate program was sufficient for his career path and could use the lessons and knowledge gained from the program to land a role in the industry. Adam is contemplating whether to return to college to finish his master's program, but chances are he will not unless he wants to attain that academic qualification. If he is happy with his job and career progression, he may not need to return to school unless he needs to attain that degree level.

The takeaway is that if you are unsure about how much education or degree you need, a good way to go about it is by breaking your degrees into 23 milestones, focusing on each step, and see how you go.

Sometimes, you do not need as much as you think, and if you find yourself comfortable and satisfied after the first milestone, then maybe you are simply good the way you are. This idea will save you some time spent in college writing exams and combining this activity with work and looking after family, but it will save you lots of money and reduce your student debts.

If you decide to go to school, check out my book "Before

Graduation Day" to learn how you can make the most of your time in school and land any role you want before graduation day.

The next part will focus on helping you continue your main or original career path as a migrant. For example, if you have worked in accounting and finance in your previous country of residence, then it is also possible to find work in this field in the new country.

Actions:

- Check if you really need to return to school before enrolling.
- Speak to other professionals in your field to understand their journey.
- Consider short top-up degrees if you need to enrol.

PART IV

——————

THE PROFESSIONAL PATH

You have made a big move to a new land.

You want to find a job and continue working in your professional career path.

What now?

How quickly you succeed in your job hunt, especially in the same field of work you worked back in your home country, depends on some factors.

Let us explore them in detail.

Confidence

You will not go far in this new world of job hunting if you do not have the confidence to job hunt, prepare your resume and cover letter and, most importantly, face an interview panel and communicate your value to them.

People can easily tell if you lack self-confidence and cannot communicate your value. Job hunting is like sales and marketing. The one who always wins is the person who has the confidence to communicate their value.

Be confident as you re-launch your professional career in a new country. Many other factors such as lack of local work experience and education may have already limited your chances of landing a role, so do not let confidence pull you down.

You will face challenges at different stages in your career, but do not let this affect your confidence when job hunting. See every challenge you face as part of your learning curve, pick up the pieces and keep going.

Strategy

Job hunting is like a game. Like games, you need a strategy to win. You need to know what the right moves are and when to take them. Timing and methodology are crucial.

This is true, especially for migrants as well. Because you are in a new country, you will find that many things are not exactly how they used to be when you were back in your home country. There are significant changes with regard to how you send applications, interview for jobs, grow your network, adjust to work cultures and how businesses function in general.

You will quickly notice that there is a lot of ground to cover. Even if you were a top professional in your home country, most of the tricks and tips you knew then might not be useful in your new country. So, knowing this gives you more understanding that you need a new strategy to land the roles you want.

You need to understand what works and what does not work when faced with new challenges. You need to redefine the steps you need to achieve your career goals. You need to learn the most effective strategies to move to the next level.

Adaptability

Drilling down from strategy, you must be as adaptable as possible in your new country, from the work culture to people relationships, languages, business jargon and the like.

Professionals who have been hugely successful in kick-starting their careers in their new destinations are those who have adapted as quickly as possible.

I remember first hearing the word "mate" in Australia. I didn't quite understand it, as it meant something else from where I came from. I quickly realised it was an informal term for friends, colleagues and the like. The more I interacted with society, the more informal words I learnt. I had to adapt as quickly as possible. When you quickly adapt to the work culture, the people and society, you will soon be seen as part of the system and one of theirs. This can influence how quickly you achieve your career goals.

A connection once posted on LinkedIn about a neighbour asking him, "How are you going?" He responded, "he was going by a train". The neighbour did not quiz further, and he wondered why. Later, he learned the phrase was more like checking how he was doing, not necessarily his transport route.

There will be business and societal jargon in your new land. Your ability to quickly adapt to the new system and way of working is crucial for your professional soft landing.

You will not learn everything overnight, but be sociable, keep learning, and adapt quickly.

RISK PROFILE

You can easily navigate your career in your destination country once you understand the limitations that might work against you.

Limitations are constraints. They are things that either consciously or subconsciously limit you from achieving your career goals. Ignoring your limitations can lead to setbacks and this can seriously limit your career progress.

One of such limitations as a migrant could be your risk profile.

When James arrived in the UK from Africa, he did not imagine it would be challenging to land a role. He was glued to his laptop, applying to several jobs online, but was unsuccessful.

While he had solid experience in his home country, there is something important he's missing and not factoring into his planning. He has not thought about whether his actions were the right step to give him the desired results.

After several no-shows, another friend asked him to speak with me. Once we jumped on the phone, I asked him one question: "Why should they hire you?".

Why you? I asked.

Why not the other person? He was quiet for a second because he could not find ready answers to that question.

While professional migrants enrich work cultures and bring vast skills and experience into the workplace, this is not immediately recognised and appreciated by most local employers. They still prefer local candidates to fill job roles, so you need to know and communicate your value to hiring managers.

Once you decide to continue the same career path as you had before you migrated to a new country, you first want to assess your risk profile. Do not just start applying without asking yourself this question. You need to know the answer to this question. What makes you stand out? As a professional, what do you bring to the table?

As simple as it is, asking yourself before committing your time and resources to job applications is important. The answers to this question will guide you through your next steps and, more importantly, on what you should focus on. They will also help you determine what you should not focus on since they are unlikely to be useful for you.

What is your risk profile?

Your risk profile is essentially the perceived risk an employer sees in you. Yes, every job seeker has a risk profile, and the successful candidate is usually the one the employer perceives as the lowest risk to them.

Why is this so?

Well, hiring is a business that involves money, time, and effort. Employers have limited resources, so they spend them wisely by employing the least risky candidate (that is, the best candidate in the pool).

Risks can be associated with credentials related to qualifications, education, skills, work experience, professional registration, local work experience, etc. The less you have compared to the next applicant, the higher your risk profile. Of course, you need to be careful not to provide false credentials that might work against you during the hiring and onboarding process.

Assume, for example, that I am applying for a data analyst role without relevant work experience, closely related degree, certification or project portfolios. My chances of getting into that role are lower than someone with these qualifications. So, the more qualifications you do not have in relation to the job description, the higher your chances of not getting hired.

So, before you start applying online and thinking about why you were not hired, you should create a risk assessment matrix to see where you stand risk-wise. Your goal is to have the lowest or no risk possible so you can be noticed and called for an interview and ultimately land the job.

When you are a new migrant, chances are you will not tick all the boxes, which is fine if you know and understand how to account for and adjust for these gaps.

Why should they hire you?

This question might sound harsh, but it urges you to start thinking about your next steps. It is an honest question that makes you think deeply about your current state.

As a recruiter, when I look at candidate profiles and resumes, I ask myself why this one and not the other person. Why A and not B? Employers will ask themselves this question on the backend, so you might as well ask yourself before applying. Failing to do so might lead to disappointments and unmet expectations.

Sometimes, we are easily attached to what we want without caring much about the employer's needs. Granted, you want a job in your professional field, and you want any job now. Yes, employers also want someone for the job; not just anyone but someone who has the qualifications and ability to carry out the responsibilities of the role.

The real question you should ask yourself is whether you fit the employer's ideal profile as the best candidate for them. Remember, it is not always about you but more about the employer and the job under consideration.

You need to analyse what risks you may be associated with before your job search process and need to find a way of resolving them. This can be through self-study or gaining a certification or work experience. Look up other candidates on LinkedIn and use the profile to gauge your situation. If it helps, you can also schedule a catch-up with them to understand their career journey.

Do not proceed without carrying out this risk analysis. Carrying out this important step will help you to be more conscious about yourself and your next steps. It will also help you channel your energy to the route where you can get the best return on investment for your applications. Remember, assess your risk, focus on your strengths and eliminate your weaknesses.

STARTING BEFORE YOU LAND

If you want to continue with your professional expertise in your field as soon as you land in your new country, you must plan and prepare before you land.

Note the keyword: before you land.

Getting started by reaching out to recruiters and applying for roles is always a great idea. You want to ensure you land some job interviews and possibly a job before you land.

When Adam landed in Canada as a new permanent resident, he had a couple of interviews with different firms the next day. It turned out that Adam had purchased a Canadian mobile number online and started applying for jobs before he landed in Canada. He was able to forward calls from his virtual Canadian mobile number to his local phone number. Upon landing, he simply attended job interviews as if he had been living in Canada and applying.

Getting an internal transfer

If your current employment from your home country is with a global company, it might be easier for you to get some sort of internal transfer to the branch in your destination country.

When Jane moved to the UK from Nigeria in 2019, she was already staffed at KPMG in Nigeria for four years and worked as a Senior Associate. Before arriving in the UK, she spoke to her managers about her intention to move to the UK and discussed possible transfers and suitable roles in the UK. Luckily, she landed another role at KPMG UK and continued her career seamlessly.

Sometimes, this route is easier and quicker. Most global companies have the same values and tend to hire individuals with similar skills across different locations. So, you should consider this option if you work with a global company with offices in your destination country. International transfers might be easier in some companies than finding a new job in a different company.

REBRANDING YOURSELF

Updating your profiles

If you are not a frequent user of LinkedIn, now is a good time to clean up your profile to reflect your work experience and brand.

Surprisingly, not many people take LinkedIn and other professional networks seriously in this modern age.

I have had countless job seekers telling me they landed roles after a recruiter noticed their profiles and contacted them directly for an opportunity. So, if you are not on LinkedIn, now is the time to create your profile on the site. Add credentials and your location to your profile.

The location feature is important as it helps the LinkedIn filtering algorithm to promote your profile to recruiters looking for job seekers in your location.

In addition to your location, you should also update other profile information, including your profile photo, about, etc. If you have not received any recommendations, you can chat with your colleagues and manager to write a nice recommendation for you on LinkedIn. We love recommendations as humans, and I bet recruiters do as well.

Take your profile photo seriously, too. It is the first thing recruiters find when they visit your profile. If you are unsure how to complete your LinkedIn profile or what information to provide, search for your job title in your proposed destination and look at the top ten candidates that pop up.

You can easily use their profile to complete your profile information as well. Chances are those candidates that pop up are well ranked based on their profile in the algorithm, so they are probably doing something right.

So, instead of wasting time thinking about what to do and what not, just grab the ten profiles and see what they have in common and try to use this guide to update your profile. Of course, be careful not to copy and paste other people's information. This might haunt you later, especially if recruiters discover that you have copied someone else's profile.

Once you get your LinkedIn profile ready, ensure your other social profiles also reflect your personality. Take a look at Twitter, Facebook, and Instagram pages. It is a good idea to tidy them up to ensure they communicate the brand you want the world to see.

Managing Your Online Persona

As you are a new migrant, your online presence or profile may contain information not highly relevant to your destination country or you may not have any online profiles at all.

I have seen top professionals suffer because of this reason. Not because they are not good but because no one notices or sees how good they are.

Sadly, we live in a gig economy, where everything is online. If you are not noticeable online or no one can tell who you are via a simple Google search, that might be a problem.

Google is your new resume.

You probably will not appreciate this need until you find yourself job hunting. The idea of job hunting has changed significantly from what it used to be. We are no longer confined to a society where the information about us is available to a limited number of people. Nowadays, anyone can know about you by looking through your online profiles and browsing your online activities. For example, if you Google my name, you will find many career development articles, data science articles, and my name on a few social media channels, and all this on the entire first search results page of Google.

The bottom line is that you need to rebrand yourself by tidying up any information about you that is available online.

Present a clear message

What do you want to communicate to the world?

This will be the first thing you should ask yourself. What do you want the world to know about you? When they think of you – what comes to mind? What do people say you are? These questions are so crucial that you need to nail them. If you do not know the answer to these questions, your online or professional brand needs more work. Like I said earlier, you need to be online. We live in a world where everyone goes online to source information and get access to almost anything they need.

You can periodically Google search your own name and check the information that comes up in search results. If any inappropriate results come up, you need to take steps to have them removed or bring up more recent, relevant information about you. Here are a few things you can do to get you going.

- Remove any negative information about you.
- Add positive information.

- Publish relevant information.

As a new migrant, you will be faced with looking for jobs. One key strategy to help you present yourself to the world and stick your name and brand out there is for you to publish information relevant to your profession or niche. Maintaining a professional image on LinkedIn can be immensely useful for job applicants. You must manage your online personas on other social networking sites as well, aligning them to your career goals.

Imagine the online media as your daily or weekly newsfeed. What do you want your readers and potential employers to see? Which roles do you want to work in? What information will be highly relevant for employers in a niche? So, once you nail down this information, you must develop a content publishing plan to make your job easier. You need a strategy. You will not sustain it long if you start without a plan, strategy or direction. Posting relevant content regularly can be cumbersome, but it increases your visibility and reach.

Having a plan helps you communicate what you should talk about, when you should talk about it, how to talk about it and to who needs to hear it.

This is what personal branding is all about.

Establishing Your Identity

It is essential to make it easy for employers and anyone to refer to you with ease, and it starts with your name. If you particularly have a long and complex name, I recommend breaking it down or using a preferred name.

My full name is "Olabanji", and while this may be easy for some people, I opted to have my preferred name "Banji" on my resume and applications. While my name may appear easy to pronounce, many names can be challenging to pronounce. Can you think of any?

Migrants can have complex names depending on their background and culture. While this is fine in your home country, it might not work well in other countries or cultures.

After a recruiter finally gives you some audience and looks at your resume or email, the last thing you want is difficulty pronouncing your name. Sadly, strong candidates can get overlooked during this process.

You want the recruiter or hiring manager to find it easy to digest your credentials and not be distracted. You want them to go straight into the main business of helping you get ahead instead of making them feel inadequate due to their inability to pronounce your name correctly.

Therefore, I encourage you to use a preferred name if you have a name that might be complex and difficult for recruiters to pronounce. They like to feel comfortable immediately, including when looking through your application.

Being Creative

You need to be creative to stand out amongst other applicants and get noticed by the recruiter. Here are a few ideas that helped my creativity.

Launching a Personal Website

A resume contains your credentials and is the key document that contains information about your suitability for a job; this is usually the first thing an employer checks after you apply for a job.

With the advent of technology, many professionals are moving online. They want to be seen or heard before a job shows up or a hiring manager requests their resume, and one way to do that is by having a personal website. Aside from your social presence and a polished LinkedIn profile, your professional resume or blog can also be online.

Besides being a repository for potential employers, your website or blog can also be an online repository for your work, achievements and key events in your personal or professional life.

Indeed, your creativity can set you apart from competitors and position you for tremendous career success.

You can look at my WordPress blog to get an idea of what a personal blog looks like. All you need is a domain name and hosting, which are usually cheap (as low as $50 per year). Take a look at my website (banjialo.com/tools) for web hosting recommendations.

The good part? Your domain name and website also come with a free custom email address.

Emailing has revolutionised how individuals communicate globally for personal and professional reasons.

Emailing will be many employers' preferred mode of communication; however, having an unprofessional email address may count against you. Emails with a username like "showme4u200" may hurt your job chances.

A typical professional email address with your name as the username (e.g., firstname.lastname@domain.com or similar) is a great way to start; however, you can do better by having a more personalised email address that comes free of charge when you buy a domain for your website. An example would be yourname@yourdomain.com instead of the standard free Google, Yahoo Hotmail, or Outlook email address.

Yes, while this may appear insignificant, it does show something unique about you, your personality and your overall profile. The additional benefit is its ability to beat the email filters set by specific organisations. Some email rules will automatically flag emails from free email providers as spam and end up in the junk folder. I once sent one of your applications in the early stages using a free email account, expecting feedback, only to realise it never reached the recruiter's inbox after I followed up. It ended up in their spam folder.

While this idea might be familiar to some professionals, especially in tech, employers in other areas would appreciate your creativity with your custom email address. Check out my website for recommendations. You do not even need to know how to build a website. You can easily hire someone on Fiverr for less than $100 to build a simple personal website for you. Give it a try! It may be one of your best career investments.

Have you been at a job too long?

Kickstart your interview and job hunt experience

Depending on how long you have been at your current job, you might find it difficult to job hunt.

From my experience, professionals who have not had to job hunt for five years or more tend to delay job search. They find it particularly challenging because they have lost their job-hunting skills.

When Andrew realised that he would be moving overseas, he realised that he had not hunted for a job for seven years. The mere thought of updating his resume, writing a cover letter, and creating an online portfolio exhausted him. He did not think he would enjoy these activities.

Andrew consulted a career coach who helped him craft a new resume and write a cover letter to get him started.

Yes, it may take a long time for you to adjust to the new realities of leaving the job in which you have worked for many years in search of another one in an unfamiliar environment. This is challenging. But you can make this less of a burden on yourself by starting your job hunt game early.

It does not matter whether you intend to take up these jobs.

What matters is that you are actively engaged in the job search and interview process. This will help you stay sharp in the job-hunting game and reduce the friction you need to start once you arrive at your new destination.

If looking for a job and occasionally interviewing is too much of a hassle, consider constantly practising your interviewing skills. You might want to consult your friends or family to act as the panel. The more practice you get in the lead time before you start interviewing properly for the jobs you want, the better your chances of achieving interviewing confidence.

I' would prefer you apply for actual jobs and engage in interviews at formal companies. That way, it can simulate the real interview process.

Building a Strong Network of Professionals

Many professionals have misunderstood the true meaning of networking. This explains why it is severely undervalued.

What does networking mean to you? Finding yourself in a large hall, about the size of a stadium, filled with strangers and exchanging business cards? Nope. Far from it. A strong network of people is that pool of human capital you can quickly tap into when you need (to exchange) ideas, information, and assistance for personal or professional reasons.

I will share a true-life story to help you understand a network's true value and meaning. A friend of mine needed a job. He contacted his network connections and let them know that he was seeking opportunities and what he wanted. After a few days, two of his connections linked him up with various jobs, and he was given another contract and settled into a new role within one week. He said he had always had this pool of people within his reach and was constantly engaging with them when he was not in need.

A strong network gives you instant access to human capital

and career resources when needed. If you do not have such a network, you might struggle a lot.

Why?

Because you can't simply tap on a stranger's shoulder and expect instant help; people help those they know and trust.

Your network is your human capital.

The more individuals you have in the circle, the more you build your career savings account, the easier it would be for you to advance your career.

Research suggests that more job positions are filled via referrals than any other route. Many jobs are not even posted online. You need to grow your network of professionals to significantly boost your chances of landing the role you wish to as a new migrant. Many jobs are filled via word of mouth.

Focus on relationships and grow your network

We are in an era where jobs now go to people not via online applications but via the backdoor. What does this mean for you? If you rely on online applications as a new migrant to land a job, chances are you are in for a long wait.

Employers give jobs to those who know. This helps them reduce their risks and the time it takes to recruit. Imagine looking through 200s of applications when you can request your staff to refer someone they know to the company. The good part is that the staff get commissions, too, in some cases, so this framework is becoming the standard across many employers. Research also shows that employees referred by a current staff also stay longer than those sources from the traditional job ad.

Leave your online applications and grow your network.

With jobs, your network is your net worth, and the more people you have in our network ready to assist you with your job search journey, the better your chances of securing a job. Of course, your network connections might not directly help you land a job. Still, they might offer informational interviews, help you with resume and cover letter reviews or refer you to their network of professionals. A network offers a main benefit: you know one professional, and this may lead to an introduction to numerous professionals in that person's professional network. So why shouldn't you take advantage of this?

Yes, I understand that this might not be the general practice in your previous country of residence, but now is the time to step out of your comfort zone and reach out to other professionals and grow your network. Again, the more people you have in your network, the higher your chances of landing your desired role. Employers hire who they know and trust, and referrals make this much easier by reducing your perceived risks, too.

Looking back at my earlier days in Australia, I got my internship and first paid job via referrals. I met these people along my study journey or via networking on LinkedIn. These people have been integral to my career as they helped me along the way by either pointing me in the right career direction or referring me to jobs that changed my career and life. So, give it a shot, leave your comfort zone, vacate your computer desk and reach out to other professionals in your field. You must find where your dream job is, and you will not know if you do not try anyway.

Your Career Coach Is Not a Magician

A friend of mine who was a new migrant woke up one day and decided a career coach was the ultimate solution to his job-hunting challenges.

He had been job hunting for a few months and wanted a shortcut to land his dream role.

He had had enough.

To him, he only needed to pay about $150 to be assured of any job he wanted in the industry.

Thankfully, he consulted with me before making the payment. I told him not to bother paying a coach yet.

He asked why.

I told him he was unlikely to find a job with his current mindset of not believing and working hard to land his dream role.

A career coach was unlikely to assist him in landing a role with his static mindset and low-energy drive.

With his high expectations from the coach, he was unlikely to put in the work required to make his job search successful.

A career coach may not solve your job-hunting challenges if you have not fixed your mindset to be ready to work and spend quality time developing quality applications for the roles you want.

I have seen many migrants pay career coaches and sleep on their job search process. They get a fine-tuned resume and cover letter from a coach to re-ignite their application power but fail to do more beyond this step.

They sometimes apply to many other jobs using the same resume without re-adapting the "magic" resume to new situations. They forget that no two job ads are ever the same.

They mistakenly assume the version of the resume or cover letter that they got from the career coach is the anointed one and should never be modified.

The result?

An underwhelming achievement from their job search.

If this is you, I am afraid a career coach may not solve your job-hunting challenges.

You need to put in the energy or effort required to keep your job search going after you have consulted a career coach.

Before reaching out to career coaches in hopes they can wave a magic wand and help you land a job, know it will not be possible if you are not ready to be committed and put in the work. You do need to be committed to get real results. Job hunting is like a job in itself.

You will have a more successful job search if you develop an accountability mindset before giving your hard-earned money to a career coach.

The job search process can be long and exhausting. It is time-consuming.

If you are unprepared to do the work, you would need more than a career coach to land a job.

Showing Your Work

Showing your work is the new way of evidencing what you can do.

Many years ago, the internet was not as popular as today. People have to ask you for lots of evidence to vet what you can do and your skills.

Today, the story has changed. Employers or hiring managers can easily find out who you are.

How?

The Internet.

Search engines are fast becoming important in recruitment. They crawl through your website as well as that of social media pages, including LinkedIn, and gather information. So, the best way to showcase your expertise in a field is to let your online presence speak for you.

You may have heard stories of professionals who were hired because they showed a skill online or wrote about something that impressed an employer. The truth is it happens quite often and will continue for many years.

Hiring is a risky business.

Employers want to be sure that you possess the necessary skills before putting you on their payroll. They want to be sure they will not spend tons of resources on you to teach you how to do your job. So, your portfolio will help you stand out.

Remember to show your work, improve your personal brand, and make it easy for employers to know what you are made of and what you can do.

There is no showing off here.

Portfolio > Resume

Show your work, build in public and position yourself for opportunities.

It works wonders.

Showing off to show up

Now and then, I put up an ad on the internet looking for someone to help me complete a task. I post in marketplaces and wait for individuals to start bidding for the service and then choose the one I believe is the right fit for me and what I am trying to accomplish.

I am sure you occasionally hire other professionals or artisans as well. This can be a graphics designer, website developer, professional branding kit, you name it.

Usually, once I receive these responses, which is generally a large number, I sit down and try to reduce the number of vendors who have indicated interest.

The first thing I ask myself is who amongst these applicants will be able to do this job.

The second step is when I ask myself: how can I know? Well, the first thing I do is to go through a list of their previous projects and reviews to see how well they performed and how satisfied their clients were. I especially check similar projects comparable to the one I am trying to accomplish to see how well they did.

Once I get a handful of people, I move on and trim it even further by looking at reviews from past sellers.

Why this story?

This is the same process employers use to shortlist candidates. The process may be slightly different, but the idea is the same. You look through a list of candidates who have applied for a job and shortlist the good ones. Then, you schedule an interview depending on the number of qualified candidates.

We are in a world where seeing is believing. And employers want to see what you can do before giving you the job. They no longer always rely on the hopes you will do the job after they give you the job. This is a fragile process because they are not sure you will be a good bet. So, one of the best ways to eliminate this risk is to ensure that your work experience is available online where employers can see it. Seeing is believing. The more similar your portfolio of work, the higher your chances of getting looked at, which reduces your risk.

Remember, hopes are not something employers want anymore. They want to be confident that you can do the job. So, depending on your profession, show your work and put your work experience online. Make a lot of noise about whatever you are working on, the results, your methods, and your thought process. Let them see it on LinkedIn since that is where most employers hang out. You do not know which of your work or projects will resonate with an employer's current problems, and then you might get an email or message to tell whether you are interested in a chat about a job opportunity.

I have seen multiple candidates get jobs via this method. I have seen employers recruit via this method. And depending on your role, this is even an absolute minimum requirement. In fields like tech, software engineering, and UI/UX, you must build a work portfolio that potential employers can see. It's no longer an option; it is a requirement. And this is now expanding to other fields.

Imagine you are trying to source a painter for your new million-dollar house. You posted this information online and received two bids. You met the bidders to chat and explore which one you could give the job to. You met with the first bidder, and he told you he could do it and that all you need is to hand him your project and the funds and that he would get started immediately and finish it for you how you like it. You would not immediately give him $ 20,000 and have him do it because something deep down within you feels incomplete.

Now imagine you met the other fellow before having a chat. He presented his portfolio to you. This had images of past painting projects in similar locations and similar clients in the same group as you. He walked you through the process, how long it took, the design and how they finished it. He even showed you a replica of what yours might look like after completion.

This may excite you, and you may want to give him a cheque on the spot to start immediately. Why? Seeing is believing. He has shown you that he can do the job well by not just word of mouth but by showing his earlier works.

Remember, do not sell hopes. Sell your work. Show your work, and you will be in the spotlight of employers. Make their job easier to find and trust you.

Why online job applications may be unsuccessful

Vee, an Indian migrant who moved to Australia, asked me whether he should apply for jobs online.

I shared my thoughts with him and will do likewise with you.

I once sent many online applications to multiple employers, hoping to get in. The magic did not happen.

Why?

I was competing with the world.

You see, any job ad that gets posted online is visible worldwide. The job posting is on the web and visible to anyone with internet access. Your grandma could see it and apply if she wanted.

For example, let us imagine I found a job ad online, and I was interested. I would be competing with the following categories of people:

- Individuals who are currently employed want to change jobs.
- Experienced individuals who recently lost their jobs.
- Those wishing to apply because they want more money.
- Internal candidates already working at that company desiring to step up.
- Friends of internal candidates who want to work with their friends.
- Your fellow migrants

As you can see, the list goes on. Some of these professionals also have local education and work experience.

So, what are your real odds of landing a job as a fresh migrant if you decide to sit on your computer all day? Have you seen why I never heard back from any of the jobs?

You will be fighting the world.

Do not get me wrong. I believe in miracles. They still happen. But when you have limited time and resources, you put your time and energy into where your odds are higher. It is smarter.

Vee was an underdog as a new migrant with limited local work experience, hence why his online job search wasn't successful.

He changed his strategy and focussed on the following:

- Followed small companies (10–100 employees) on LinkedIn.
- Reached out to staff working in preferred roles to learn about their work.
- Reached out to friends and family and professional network about potential opportunities (yes, they do work!)
- Attended small networking events like Meetups.
- Contacted recruitment agencies.

Once he did this, he started gaining traction, leading to a job offer.

Of course, some exception occurs. Your odds are higher if applying online for positions with mass recruitment exercises — think of those consulting firms having annual recruitment events where they hire many professionals. Your odds are also higher if you live where skilled workers are scarce. You get the point. Do not spend so much time applying online, especially if you have done that for some time with no results.

Always evaluate your job search process, remove what is not working for you and focus on what works. The more you can remove the unproductive process and focus on the method that works, the higher your chances of landing your first job as a new migrant.

WHY ONLINE APPLICATIONS CAN BE INEFFECTIVE

Another reason to be wary of online applications is that they are sometimes outdated. Employers might have already filled the position and forgotten to remove the online application from the job site.

This happens often, so the fact that you see a job online does not mean it is still active, so understand that a job position you find online may not always be available.

A friend of mine moved to Canada in 2022. Searching for job opportunities online, he found a role that suited him. He applied immediately and was ecstatic, as if he had landed the job. When he told me about it, I asked him to contact the company or the hiring manager to learn more about the role. He followed my advice. He was surprised when the hiring manager told him that the job had been filled six months ago. The company had not removed the job posting from the website. While he felt disappointed that the role that he aspired for had been filled, he was also now clear that the position was unavailable and did not pin his hopes on it.

If you are a new migrant, I would not recommend online applications. Exceptions are if you are highly skilled in your field, have considerable work experience in a top organisation, and have proof to back up your case. The reason I saw this is that most times, online applications do not work for most people. Some find it to be too much work with too little return.

But if you must apply online, contacting the company or the hiring manager is a great idea. The result of the conversation may turn out to be more helpful than you imagine.

UNFAMILIAR JOB TITLES

Job positions and titles vary across many regions and countries. Sometimes, this confuses migrants and makes them miss good opportunities. For example, when I first arrived in Australia, I saw roles such as Customer Success Manager or Customer Experience Manager. These titles did not make sense to me at first. I wondered whether there were new kinds of roles in this part of the world. However, when I read the job descriptions, roles and responsibilities, I realised that they are the same as Customer Service Manager roles; only the job title had been tweaked a little.

Your focus should be on tasks and responsibilities, not job titles. If you can do the job, make sure you go for it and do not let the difference in titles stop you. In addition, you may want to reference the job title they have written and presented since that is their business jargon or industry jargon and to get past the ATS system if they have one in place.

Remember, your focus should be on the job and responsibilities rather than titles. If you can add value and believe you are the right fit, I encourage you to go for it. You only need to meet 50–60% of the requirements, including the core requirements. You do not have to meet all the requirements.

Job titles should not be the impediment that will make you ignore the job you want.

Tasks, responsibilities, and role fit are what employers care about. This is more important to them than just job titles. They understand job titles change across companies, industries, and regions, so do not let this limit you when you find a role you love.

APPLYING FOR A JOB

Resume and cover letter formats

The resume and the cover letter are not going away any time soon. I do not know how these two documents have managed to survive the test of time despite the advent of technology and the shift in working methods.

We can be sure that you will need these documents to apply for a job. Knowing this, you must craft them well. Your resume, which lists your credentials, is your marketing tool.

I have seen numerous resume formats. I will not go too deep into this, but the first thing you need to do is to look online for a good resume format in your new country. You will find tons of resume formats online. If you have contacts in your new country, it is also a good idea to either request a copy of their resume or ask them to review your current resume. That way, you will be sure this document is of acceptable quality.

Resume formats can differ, and you will need to quickly adapt to what is working in your region to get noticed by employers. For example, it is customary for job seekers in my home country to include personal information such as date of birth, local area, marital status, and the like on their resume. However, I quickly learned that in Australia and similar countries, you do not need to provide such information. Thankfully, upon arrival, I requested free resume samples from my connections and a free resume review service. So, create a good resume and keep it professional.

As this is the first document an employer asks for and it is the first impression you make on the employer, having a resume ready is a must. When someone asks for your resume or when you see a job posting, you will be able to respond as soon as possible. The earlier you share your resume with the recruiter, the better your chances of landing the job that you want.

Preparing for the interview

I had never realised interviews could be challenging for some candidates until recently. I experienced firsthand why migrants struggle to ace job interviews.

You can be the best candidate with the best skills in the world, but if you fail to convince the panel by telling the story and communicating your value, you may not land the job.

Do not keep job interview preparation to the last minute too!

I wonder why some candidates keep interview preparation to the very last minute, hoping that they can wing it. While some can accomplish this successfully, the best candidates often take time to prepare for job interviews. That said, you will need to prepare thoroughly for your interview. Please do not take it lightly. Interviewing as a new migrant is often more difficult. You must convince the panel that you know the job, can do the job, and understand the organisation, country, social norms, and the likes. As you can see, there are more gaps to fill.

As a new migrant, if you have an upcoming interview, it

may also be best to consult with a trusted friend or colleague who has been around for longer and understands what local employers require. You want to get a few dot points on how to prepare best and ways to come out as a great candidate.

Interviewing can be challenging for new migrants.

When James arrived in Canada from Africa, he was introduced to a company via a recruitment agency. He was scheduled for an interview with a company representative in no time. He was excited at this opportunity and hoped to impress the panel. He hopes to land this role only after a few weeks in Canada. The interview did not go very well based on his feedback. The company realised he was fresh from another part of the world and would need more on-the-job training to get him up to speed. While some companies will be ready to invest in new hires, depending on the role, other companies do not want to do this at all. They want to hire someone who understands the job, the work culture, and the organisation and can hit the ground running as soon as possible.

So, I encourage you to start interviewing formally or informally as soon as possible. If it helps, you should also engage a local career coach who will teach you exactly what you need to interview successfully in your new country since it may be quite different from what you are used to. At the minimum, you must prepare well for the interview and communicate your value. Do not assume you will just go in and wing it.

You need to learn to communicate your value.

While most migrants are brilliant in what they do, they fail to comprehend that interviewing is a selling process. Sadly, not many understand how to sell themselves by communicating their value to employers. Employers can quickly detect when a candidate lacks confidence or cannot adequately communicate their value.

Even if you are a great candidate and cannot communicate

your value, then it might be challenging for the panel to see your value and understand your worth.

I have seen excellent candidates looked over, and average candidates selected over the excellent ones. Why? The excellent candidates did not communicate their value adequately. Sadly, interviews are judged mostly based on performance, especially when interviewing alongside other candidates. Your success lies mostly in how well you did at the interview. That is how you will be ranked against the other candidates.

So, polish your interviewing skills before your first job interview and always prepare for upcoming job interviews.

Being creative with your job search

If you are not used to thinking outside the box to land jobs, now is the time to make that happen.

Why?

Because it is often possible that you will land jobs via your other means outside traditional online applications.

When Theresa landed in Australia, she did not quite know what she could do with her law degree. She looked online and realised she had to take professional exams before getting a job.

Unfaced by this daunting requirement, she decided to take her job search into her lands. She noticed a small business close to her home. She often passed by this small business whenever she went shopping.

One day, she approached the business owner, stating her background and how she could add value to their work. Without thinking twice, the business owner hired her on the spot and asked her to start work as soon as possible. Theresa has since worked in top companies in Australia and attributes her success to the opportunity she received in her early days.

Sometimes, it takes creative and non-traditional ways to get your first job. Do not be limited to applying online. Chances are that most people are doing the same too! So why limit yourself to this approach?

Similarly, when James landed in Australia with his Chemistry degree from Africa, he did not quite know how best to approach his career search in a new country. He has heard stories of how difficult it was to land jobs if you did not have the traditional local experience and degree in Australia. Having worked in his home country for a few years, he knew he could land something he loved. After unsuccessful rounds of online applications and no-shows, he decided to take things into his own hands. He targeted specific companies he was interested in and started making connections with those companies. In no time, he was invited for a chat, which ended up being a job offer.

Job applications have no boundaries, so you should not box yourself with popular job sites. Learn to go out of your way and apply to any job you are interested in using non-traditional means. Chances are you will still face rejections, but often, all you need is one yes. Remember, it is best to keep working consistently towards your goal because you do not know when the YES will come. You will get what you want in the end.

Interning and Volunteering

I have seen professional migrants opt for volunteer and internship work experience upon arrival in a new country. This category believes local work experience is crucial for them, and they do not mind spending a couple of months to find a paid or unpaid job, provided it will help them put one foot in the door.

When Sam arrived in Sydney as an Engineer, he did not waste any time at all in spending lots of time applying for jobs online. He wanted to enter the market as soon as possible with little or no friction. While his colleagues focused on online job applications, he went the other way, contacting potential companies of interest and asking for volunteer/internship positions. He did not care whether it was paid or unpaid. All he knew was he needed to get his foot in the door, and the rest would be fine. He also believed his little finances would seem his through the unpaid period until he could find paid work.

Luckily, Sam quickly secured a role as an engineer in a small firm in Sydney. Soon, his employers noticed his skills and talents, and they offered him a job offer once a position came up in their organisation.

Ultimately, it paid off for Sam, as you can see. Sometimes, an internship or volunteer position can help unlock potential job opportunities by helping you get your foot in the front door. Any good employer who notices your skills and talents will look for ways to retain you. Employers want talent and understand that these talents can be scarce in the market, so why let the current talent leave if you have current openings?

I have added this point because sometimes, volunteering experience may be the way to go. There has been debate about whether candidates should take up unpaid volunteering or internships. I will not be dwelling on that here. If you want to explore without impacting your finances, especially if it is unpaid, you should explore it and look for paid jobs. And who knows, sometimes, employers may also pay you for your work, so do not delay. Look out for the next volunteering opportunity; this may be important in your career. Remember, volunteering does not have to be full-time. You can go part-time too and have more days to yourself to look for paid work if your current opportunity is unpaid.

Gaining local experience

Volunteering and internship opportunities can quickly help you bridge the gap in your local experience inadequacies. Most paid jobs value candidates who have some local work experience. They do not care whether it is an internship, volunteer, or paid work. They want experienced candidates because they believe they have interfaced with the system and will understand how it works.

So, volunteering may be the way to go if you are quickly looking for local work experience to bridge your experience gaps.

Meeting other professionals

Volunteer and internship opportunities can be a way to meet other professionals in your field. Finding someone else to speak your business jargon and learning from them to bridge any knowledge gap can be helpful.

Volunteering can be a way to do this quickly if you want to meet other professionals as soon as possible in a work setting. You may get referrals for future opportunities too.

Gaining soft skills and understanding the work culture

Most employers are not confident in hiring overseas workers because they may not understand the work culture. Work culture is about how things work in society, which can be different from how things work from where you migrated from. For example, it is customary to use "Sir" and "ma'am" where I came from if you speak to your bosses, but I quickly realised it was unnecessary in Western countries.

Volunteering can give you the exposure you need to understand the new society.

Reducing the risk profile

Employers prefer to hire candidates they perceive as having low risk: those with the right experience, right skills, right mindset, right domain or background, and education. A hiring manager wants candidates who tick all or most of these boxes. The more boxes you tick, the higher your chances of landing a role. It is not just with migrants; this is how recruitment works generally.

Gaining local work experience via volunteering or internships can significantly reduce perceived risks and can improve your visibility to employers.

An internship or volunteer opportunity can also provide you with the stepping stone you need to land the job you want simply by getting your foot in the right door. Do not rule out this possibility since it may make an enormous difference in your career in the new land.

Focusing on the goal

Remember, no matter how challenging your early start is, keeping an eye on your primary goal is essential. Yes, this may sound funny, but there will be days you will be discouraged and lose focus on your primary goal, which is to land your dream job. There will be days when you think you made the wrong decision to move to a new country. There will be days when you will question your choices and wish you were not doing what you are doing now. There will be those low days. It does not happen just to you. It happens to almost everyone. I also had doubts in my initial stages. I wondered whether I made the right move in the first place. I questioned my own decisions. What matters is for you to keep sight of the goal no matter how challenging. Do not be distracted. Keep chasing your dream. Make plans for yourself and put your goal first.

Remember, even if you work in a role that you do not admire, you should create time to reward yourself by planting seeds towards your own future. Take action every day towards your goal. As the saying goes, tough situations do not last long but tough people do. You will eventually find your place and a career that works for you if you do not give up.

Don't give up on your job search

Job search can be unpredictable and can take time.

Like everything else, the more you try, the higher your chances of success.

For example, if you tried to learn a new skill and only committed one hour per week, your odds of mastering that skill are significantly lower than someone who does it daily for four hours.

More consistent and focused action leads to higher chances of results.

It is similar to a job search, too. You need to put in more effort to increase your odds of getting the desired results.

Treating Job Hunting as a Job

Job hunting is a job in itself.

You need to treat your job search like you have a job.

What do I mean by that?

You must get up daily and dedicate a specific time to your job search.

For example, if you are free in the early hours, spend a couple of hours every morning on your job search.

Of course, you do not have to send your resumes online for the duration of the period—any step you take to advance your job search counts towards the entire process.

This activity could be growing your network online or researching a company. The key message is to dedicate a specific number of daily hours to looking for work.

You may ask, but how many hours is sufficient to commit to this process?

Well, it depends on your situation. Ideally, if you need a job like your life depends on air, then be prepared to dedicate several hours daily to your job search. Take breaks when needed, of course.

The more urgent you need to land the role, the more hours you should put in. As I said, looking for work is a job, so be prepared to dedicate quality time.

Looking for a job can be daunting for many migrants. Not that there are no jobs, but more because it can take time to find one. You can't quench your thirst with a few drops of water.

The more time you strategically dedicate to your job search, the higher your chances of landing the desired role. Do your part.

Your career is a journey

The good news is that you only need to do this at the initial stages of your career.

Your job search process tends to become considerably easier once you have some work experience. At this point, you have understood the new work culture and adapted to society, so you are more like a local.

The first job is usually the most challenging of all. Once you break this barrier and land your first role, things become easier, even when applying online. Now, you have the necessary skills required by most employers and can confidently apply online and compete with other candidates in the pool.

These days, I go right in and apply online. Why? I have solid work experience that will catch the eye of any employer.

Job hunting in a new land can be challenging at the initial moments. Once you break this barrier by landing your first role, things become easier with landing subsequent roles.

· · ·

Actions:

- Kickstart your job search efforts as early as possible.
- Expand your network and connect with like-minded professionals.
- Rebrand yourself and use creative ways to land the job you want.

PART V
______

THE ENTREPRENEUR PATH

Building on the side

You can also create a job for yourself if you have the energy and mindset. However, I would like to add a caveat that this process can be slow and unsuitable, especially if you urgently need a source of income. Even if you need a source of income, you can still commit a few hours per week to do this on your own. The benefits are huge.

I have seen professionals who just committed a few hours to doing something they love and focusing on their work become full-time entrepreneurs later.

Taking stock of your skills

If you are looking to earn money, you need skills or knowledge in an area to teach others. To earn money, you need to offer some service to others who need it. So, the first thing you want to do is to take stock of your skills. You do not have to be an expert. You just must be good enough to teach others something that you already know, provided there is a market for it.

I hired a WordPress developer who built a simple WordPress site for me. He charged about $100. It was a big amount for him, as he lived in a low-income country.

After a couple of jobs and referrals, I asked him how he started developing websites. He said all he did was watch a 2–3-hour video on YouTube, and that was it. He has probably made over $500 from me alone within six months. I am sure he is doing well. He would be paying for his bills conveniently if he has other returning customers like me. His rates are even higher now. He started charging more money as he improved his skills.

So, the bottom line is that you should be ready to learn some skills. That is how you make money.

Using social media

Once you decide to make money by offering your skills, it is a good idea to start building a following on social media. This will help you test some initial ideas and see what resonates with your audience. You do not need to have a personal audience of your own. You just need to leverage social media where you know your existing audience normally hangs out. A good example is LinkedIn since employers also hang out there as well.

Do not worry too much about the quality of your posts. Just do it. You will begin to receive feedback and learn from the process.

Starting small

All you need is to start small. You do not need fancy tools

and do not have to buy expensive tools to start building on the side. You probably have all you need to get started – the number one requisite is your willingness to get started. Once you meet this requirement, everything else becomes easier.

So how do you start?

By creating useful content and teaching others with the assumption that you already have a job.

Creating content has two main forms – text and video. Depending on what you love to do, you only have to do one of them. For example, I feel more comfortable writing than speaking on camera, so you will probably find more of my content in writing format than in video form.

You must decide what works best for you and stick to it by committing to publishing informative content once every week using your skills. It is highly beneficial if this content is also aligned with your occupation. Employers and other professionals like you can notice your work and engage your services.

Registering a business

You may choose to continue showing your skills online informally as a hobby. But if you want to formalise this process, you must get a business name. A business name is the legal name you register for your business. You do not need a unique or fancy name. Your name will be sufficient.

The key benefits of having a business name are that it can add professionalism, help create a brand and make marketing initiatives effective. You must plan for this scenario, as it will be helpful when your side hustle grows into a full-fledged business in the future.

A business name in Australia costs about $40 per year, which is quite affordable. This amount may vary in the country that you are in, but they are not likely to be expensive.

. . .

Generating content

Write about what you know on Twitter and LinkedIn every day. Do not worry too much about the other social networking sites. You will be overwhelmed trying to post everywhere. The goal is to focus on popular marketplaces where potential employers can find you. From my knowledge, Twitter and LinkedIn are the best two, so post daily and remember to engage with the comments and questions you receive.

Offering services on marketplaces

Once you build momentum on social media and constantly post content, you want to provide services on marketplaces like Upwork and Fiverr. Don't worry too much about money at this stage. The idea is to start with minimum barriers to entry. Look at other sellers offering similar services, check out their costs and go slightly cheaper.

Once you get your initial clients, ensure you do an awesome job for a good review to be posted on your profile. Once you get more clients, you can increase your rates and see how the market reacts. You will begin to make a bit more money than when you just started.

Polishing your skills

As with everything else, you need to keep growing your skills. You will need to immerse yourself in thorough study and learning to keep improving. The goal is to become confident in your skills in 6–12 months. Read resources. Use some of your income to buy quality paid resources if you need to. Remember, the best person you can ever invest in is yourself.

. . .

Creating products

Once you become comfortable learning your skill, creating simple products to teach others what you know and have learned is a good idea. You can make simple products like eBooks, short video courses, a paid community of learners you teach, one-on-one consultations and other products hosted on your website. Do not think this step too much; do your best and move on to the next thing.

Landing a job (if you still need one)

Okay, back to the original story. If you still need the job, this is a better time to get one. By this time, you would have developed excellent skills, built a portfolio of work, built a good following on social media, received reviews, and become more confident in your abilities to land a job. Chances are you may not need it. Keep gaining skills, build a work portfolio on social media, get a couple of customers by offering free services and then start providing services on marketplaces.

Don't just wait for a job. Challenge yourself and create a job for yourself while waiting.

Benefits of going on your own

Getting noticed by potential employers

One main benefit of publishing content out there is that you begin to attract potential employers. Remember why they did not hire you in the first place and why you could not get interviews? Because your risk profile was high. You will automatically lower your risk profile once you begin to publish useful content. Besides, publishing content has made it easier for employers to notice you. Often, you may be even approached by people already working in the job you want to work at. They may ask you a question or two about a process, and you begin to boost your network before you know it. Remember, the more people you have in your network, the better and the higher your chances of landing a role.

You begin to amass career evangelists who will support your work and possibly refer you to their own company if an opportunity arises. Why? They have seen firsthand that you can do the job, and you have just made it easy to be hired by employers.

Remember, creating useful content can be a way to attract employers and opportunities and, subsequently, the job you want. I have seen and heard stories on LinkedIn of how content creation led to job offers. So do not stop here thinking you can't do anything at all with your life. Don't just submit online applications and wait for the perfect job. Be creative in your own way, start creating content and lead the way. The jobs will come to you.

Reducing your risk profile

Have you submitted tons of online applications and never heard back?

Maybe it is because your risk profile is high, and employers or hiring managers think you would not be a good fit for the role.

You can easily reduce or eliminate these risks by creating useful content before potential employers. Why? The fact that you have shared knowledge by creating tons of useful content related to your profession shows you are skilled and ready to commit to developing yourself.

Employers love this eagerness and willingness, and you will be their main candidate once they realise how good you are and how better you can become on the job. If you can do this while being unpaid, you can do even more when you get paid.

. . .

Earning an income

My developer connection on Twitter (now X) went from being a software engineer to writing full-time. He has written for individuals and businesses and charges an average of USD 750 per content. He now works for himself full-time writing. He no longer works 9–5. How did it start? He took writing as a hobby and started to write about software engineering. In no time, his blogs started attracting readers worldwide and getting paid to write for others.

When you choose this route, chances are you will be approached by individuals and companies that need your services, and you will start earning for your work. The best part is that you already have your business name registration, taxes, and everything else set up, so you will be ready to hit the ground running.

Do not ignore this route especially if you are highly skilled in the tech space. Create useful content and employers may come chasing after you and you may not need a 9–5 job anymore.

Attracting loyal readers or viewers

When you create content online, others are reading or viewing your work. Your content, in turn, helps others, and you will, in turn, attract readers you never knew existed.

When I started writing online, it was all for fun, not until I started receiving emails from readers I never met or imagined who showed support.

Of course, not everyone will appreciate what you do. It doesn't matter at all. Your goal is to focus on those that will read and find value in your work. I have also somehow developed a loyal audience who reads my work, proofreads, and provides feedback on my work, especially when I have made an error. They are kind enough to point out my mistakes and suggest better ways to do things.

Keeping your resume updated

Resume gaps are not fun. Employers do not like them.

I have seen the best candidates questioned about career gaps in their resumes. The truth is that life happens, and there are more reasons now than ever for career gaps. This could be being made redundant due to a restructuring, the impact of COVID-19, taking a break or, in your case, moving to a new location.

The truth is that it can take some time to find your foot in your new country.

A quick way to circumvent this problem is to keep yourself busy by publishing useful content online and by offering your services to individuals and businesses who might need your skills. The best part is that you can then include this side hustle on your resume as work experience.

Improving your communication skills

A good way to improve your communication skills is by publishing useful content. When I started writing more consistently after about six months, I could tell my writing skills had improved from when I first started. When I look at the pieces of content I wrote in the early days, I wonder if I wrote them all. They do not look great to me.

The truth is that your initial pieces of content will not look as great, but chances are no one will see them or even care about them. These are your stepping stones to getting better and improving your writing, speaking, listening, and reading skills.

When you create content, you put your writing, speaking, listening and reading skills into play. The best part? These skills are transferrable and will be useful to you in your job.

Developing Strong Entrepreneur Spirit and Skills

You will become self-motivated and an excellent problem solver when using your skills to earn and make a living. These are life skills that will be crucial for your career success.

You will have a strong self-belief in terms of being able to learn and become great at anything if you put in the time and effort.

Landing a job

You will likely find job offers and side gigs when you constantly produce helpful content for global audiences.

Creating content can easily help you get noticed and get a job. I have seen many LinkedIn connections doing this and landing the job they want. It is the number one route that I recommend to job seekers. The steps are quite simple: pick a platform, a content type, and stick to a regular routine.

Creating content is one of the easiest ways to get noticed and land any job you want in that niche.

Becoming incredible and unstoppable

Imagine the energy that comes into landing and starting a job after going through this challenging moment and running your show all day and night? You will perform incredibly well at your next job.

You become an all-rounder because you must learn several things to wade through the challenges.

You will become a high-flyer.

Most entrepreneurs are superhumans.

Not landing a job may be disappointing, but it can also be a terrific opportunity to inspire yourself and others around you.

HARNESSING YOUR HIDDEN TALENTS

Migrating to a new country gives you a fresh perspective on your career. For example, you may have taken up a job in banking in your home country because that was what was available then. Or because there were not many opportunities for you, so you had to take up the best one among those available.

Have you always loved creative art, cooking or designing but did not have any opportunity to use such a skill? Did you stick to your banking job to earn an income?

The good news is that once you migrate to another destination country, chances are you can pick up and develop those extra skills that you could not put to good use.

So, if you've ever been passionate about any specific skills, consider growing those skills and finding a job in which they are highly valued.

Turning your passion into your profession

When Chanel arrived in Australia from Africa, all she was thinking about was how to get back into school to study nursing to find work in healthcare. She enrolled into the university and spent three years completing her nursing degree. After she completed her degree, she started a job in that field.

However, she noticed she had great cooking skills and often spent time cooking for clients who would not stop contacting her to offer her paid services to prepare various meals for them.

She spent after-work hours and weekends completing these orders, yet it was as if there was not enough time to serve her customers. The orders kept coming, and so was the cash.

After a few weeks, she decided to go part-time at work since more and more orders kept coming. She truly enjoyed cooking and was able to do it without stress. And she had the comfort of her home and her cooking tools.

Despite working part-time, she was still overwhelmed with food orders from new and returning customers. She made significantly more money from cooking meals than from her role as a nurse.

After a few weeks, she quit her nursing job to focus exclusively on cooking. She genuinely enjoyed cooking and was able to do it without stress.

Today, she no longer thinks about her nursing job. She has more paying customers both in her local community and interstate. She makes a considerable amount of money, and the margin is great.

Why this story?

Sometimes, you may think all you need to survive is a formal education and a 9–5 job. As you can see from this example, your passion can quickly turn into your profession if you can use your existing skills to provide services to those around you. If you have great handy skills with a good market, you may want to consider starting something on the side to see how it goes.

You will be surprised how much you can earn using your

side skills, which you can ultimately take up full-time. Your skills or hobby can eventually turn into your full-time career.

Aside from this fellow, I have seen other professionals who went from side hustle to becoming a full-time gig. A popular YouTuber, Ali Abdaal, also became a full-time YouTube creator after leaving his job as a doctor in the NHS.

He shared insightful stories about his journey. You can easily look up his videos on YouTube. There are so many other successful solopreneurs who used their existing skills to power businesses. The key is for you to pay attention to your other skills or talents. These skills can change your life forever.

Using your skills for your own company

When Julius arrived in the US, he planned to get an engineering-related job and start where he left off in his home country. He imagined doing this engineering job and retiring for good.

Once he joined healthcare and stayed on the job for a few years, he realised he had more passion for healthcare. Working in the sector had allowed him to understand the sector so well.

After a few years of working with the organisation, he decided it was time to set up his company.

Everyone thought this idea was crazy when he first started. They wondered how he was going to get clients and how he would support himself financially.

Julius did not care anyway. He pulled resources and started this new company. Three years on, Julius has been doing well with his new company. He has also hired over fifty staff who helped run the company.

Why this story?

Sometimes, you may build new skills due to a role or job you picked up because you could not find a job in your preferred work area.

Rather than feeling sorry for yourself or bad about how

your plans have not worked out, you should focus on learning new skills and understanding the sector. You never know. It may be a new area in which you may develop a deep interest, allowing you to build something of your own.

Like Julius, you may develop novel ideas or innovative approaches to do something differently. This idea may make you stand out from your competitors when you start your own company.

So, do not be afraid to learn or work in a new sector. Get involved and look around you for innovative ideas you can test and validate. Who knows where your new idea may lead? All it takes is one new idea at the right place and time to fulfil your potential.

Benefits of going on your own

I know getting a 9–5 job and joining the city life can be appealing. That is what most people do. You find work that pays the bills and remain on autopilot until retirement.

The truth is that there is nothing bad with this approach. However, you do not have to follow this path. If you possess the right skills, tools and mindset, there is plenty to do. Customers will always need services. And if you find yourself being able to provide what people need, you may be able to make money without stress and enjoy other numerous benefits below.

Freedom

When you are on your own, you have freedom. We all love the freedom to be our own boss and not to answer to anyone else. It is appealing. When you work for yourself, you have total freedom.

So, if you have the skills and the zeal to be on your own,

especially if you have customers coming your way, go for it and do not look back.

More earnings

Of course, one of the perks of working for yourself is that you can decide what rates to charge. Business owners earn far more than most people who work for others. So, if you possess the right skills and mindset and have the potential to serve a sizeable number of customers, then you might be set for a smooth career journey.

Flexibility

The COVID-19 pandemic has shown that we desire more flexibility. Many want to spend more time at home with their family. Having your own business can be the avenue to make that happen. So, before displacing those old skills you have thinking they will not be useful and instead chasing life in the 9–5 work, you also want to explore this option.

Remember, your reach as a business owner or entrepreneur is limitless. You have numerous customers to observe. Do not look back if you believe you have the right skills and tools. Go for it. Not everyone will be suited for a 9–5 job.

Fulfilment

Building something incredible and solving real-life problems can be fulfilling for most professionals. If you are up for it, do not discard the idea of getting the rewards of building something you own and fulfilling your lifelong dreams.

Actions:

- You do not have to follow the traditional 9-5 career path.
- Take stock of your skills.
- Be ready to launch your own venture by using your skills to provide value to others.

PART VI

CONCLUSION

Finding what works for you – no two people are the same

For a migrant, settling in a foreign land can be challenging. No two migrants will ever have the same experiences. As a new migrant, you will face some initial challenges, such as finding the right accommodation for yourself, finding a good school for your kids and finding suitable employment. What works for you might not work for someone else, and vice versa. A career that is perfect for me might not be suitable for you.

Knowing this, it is important to find and stick to what works for you. Remember that you are unique and one of a kind. No other person has the same physiological and psychological make-up as you. No other person has the same skills and interests as you. Your career choice must align with your own skills, passions and values.

Moving forward

While settling in a foreign land, adapting to a new environment is the biggest challenge. Learning the ways of life in the new country is the most essential first step to move forward. You must learn the customs and practices of your new country. You must learn the local language, the work culture, and the laws of the new land. And then you must find the opportunities for your growth and decide on a suitable career to give you the life you want.

Most challenges are temporary. They will disappear if you tackle them with the right attitude and mindset. The initial weeks or months might be challenging, but you can wade through them if you have a positive mindset.

No matter what obstacles you find ahead of you, keep going. Develop the ability to bounce back from your initial setbacks and keep working towards your career goals. Always remember your original plan. The reason that made you migrate in the first place. Your vision made you jump into the plane either alone or with your family to embark on a new career journey.

Keep moving ahead no matter what happens. Remember that challenges will not last forever and that they are a normal part of any career journey.

Finding a mentor

No matter how far you go in your career journey, you still need someone to guide you. You need a mentor, no matter how good you are and how well you think you can advance without help. Good mentors will guide you through crucial career decisions and help avoid pitfalls that you might have encountered had you travelled unaided in your career journey.

Do not go alone. Life as a new migrant in a new country is

challenging. Sometimes, travelling with good people can make the journey easier and more enriching. That said, make sure you surround yourself with people whose mission and vision are similar to yours. This will make you remain focused, especially during challenging times.

For any professional, having a good circle of mentors is always a great idea. Mentors can help you clarify your career goals, provide specific insights, help you set goals, maintain accountability and provide valuable references.

Getting help

Launching your career as a new migrant can be daunting. Remind yourself that you do not have to do this alone. You probably know a person who has been in the country for a longer time. Even if you did not, you can search and find online a community of professionals with similar backgrounds and interests as yours. Becoming a member of such a community can benefit you in many ways, such as expanding your network, learning about your industry trends and growing as a professional.

When situations turn difficult, get help when you need it. Ask for clarifications whenever you need them. Seek help from those who have crossed similar adverse situations. You do not need to make the same mistakes that others before you had made. Human interactions can help you navigate unknown journeys, ensuring your health, social, and mental well-being.

Not everyone will help. Not everyone will readily lend you a hand. Some professionals are wary of other people, so do not take it personally if you do not get help from some of them. Remember that not everyone will help you, but some people will. You only need to focus on those who will help you rather than worry about others who do not take your calls.

Doing your research

Coming off from the above point, no matter what you already know or have been told to do, remember to do your research. Do not rely on words alone if someone provides you with career advice; endeavour to do your search. I have seen migrants take wrong career steps because they received bad career advice. They adopted the advice without verifying the facts and whether the information was helpful to their personal situation.

I am not saying you should not listen to career advice from others but do so carefully and verify any information or advice you receive. It is better to be doubly sure before taking any major step. You also want to take advice from people with first-hand experience. Free advice is cheap. Sadly, not all pieces of advice are worth following. Some are great, while others are not good. The advice was probably given with the right intentions. Everyone tries to help but this help comes from in the form of differing opinions and advice.

Ask for help, verify the facts before making an important career decision and preferably speak to those with firsthand experience and have faced a similar situation.

Share what you know with others.

I hope that you settle in as quickly as possible, not just for yourself and for the sake of your family, but also to help other professionals. Yes, new migrants will find and contact you for information or clarification. Endeavour to share what you know with others. Many great minds inform a community, so always be ready to collaborate and help.

Remember, every step you take, no matter how challenging, is a step towards building a successful career in your new home.

I wish you the best.

FURTHER READING

This book was inspired by some amazing reads. Here are other inspiring books you should consider reading:

- *Navigating Change* – Niyi Borire
- *What Color Is Your Parachute* – Richard N. Bolles
- *Show Your Work* – Austin Kleon
- *Steal Like an Artist* – Austin Kleon
- *Atomic Habits* – James Clear

ACKNOWLEDGEMENT

Thanks to Dr Niyi Borire, a Neurologist, Speaker and Change Agent for the insights I gained from his amazing book. Check out his book "`Navigating Change" to learn about his career journey as a migrant.

I would also like to thank Pan Perera, Founder of Elevar Career Coaching, for his contributions. Pan helps migrants land their dream jobs. Find out more about Pan at https://www.elevardigital.com

YOUR FREE GIFT

As a buyer of this book, you will receive exclusive access to Pan's premium 20 must-have email templates.

Pan is a career expert who helps migrants land any job they want.

These templates will help you follow-up confidently and win more job offers.

Get your copy for FREE at www.pan.banjialo.com

Want to learn more about Pan's work and how he can help you achieve your career goals as a migrant? Visit https://www.elevardigital.com/ immediately.

A SIMPLE REQUEST

Thank you for reading this book.

I have a simple request. If you enjoyed this book, I would be grateful if you could leave a 5-star review. It will only take a minute or two of your time, but it will mean a lot to me because every review counts.

Remember, you don't have to use your real name if you don't feel comfortable doing so.

Thank you.

Banji Alo

ABOUT ME

Thank you for purchasing this book. I hope you found this book helpful. My goal has been to support you and provide you with the information you need to advance your career.

My name is Banji Alo. I am currently living in Australia. I work full-time in data analytics. However, I spend my free time reading books and resources on career development, psychology, productivity, and career growth and often share my thoughts with the world.

I enjoy engaging with professionals like you because I want to help you advance your career.

If we are not connected on social media yet, I encourage you to look at the links at the end of this page so we stay connected.

Do not forget to give this book a 5-star review if you enjoyed the content. You can also contact me directly at <u>banji@banjalo.com</u> if you have questions.

Remember to download your exclusive gift at https://pan.banjialo.com.

Find me on social media and let us keep the conversation going.

ALSO BY BANJI ALO

Before Graduation Day - Get The Best Out of Your Tuition And Land Your Dream Job